C000127842

CONTEMPORARY QUILTS
FROM
TRADITIONAL DESIGNS

Contemporary Quilts From Traditional Designs

Caron L. Mosey

E. P. DUTTON   NEW YORK

(Frontispiece, page ii). Detail from *October Landscape* by Susan Locher, Tallmadge, Ohio. The complete quilt is illustrated on page 5.

Book design by Marilyn Rey.

/Published in the United States by E. P. Dutton, a division of NAL Penguin Inc., 2 Park Avenue, New York, N.Y. 10016. /Published simultaneously in Canada by Fitzhenry and Whiteside, Limited, Toronto. / W / Library of Congress Catalog Card Number: 87-71372. / Printed and bound in Spain. / ISBN: 0-525-24568-5 (cloth); ISBN: 0-525-48336-5 (DP).
10 9 8 7 6 5 4 3 2 1 First Edition

In memory of my grandparents
George and Edith Covert
and
Joseph and Estelle Ryan

ACKNOWLEDGMENTS

Since I began working on this book in early 1985, I have been very fortunate to have come in contact with many quilt lovers across the United States who were willing to share their quilts, knowledge, and photograph collections with me. Special thanks go to Joyce Aufderheide, Cuesta Benberry, Nancy Dice, Jean Eitel, Flavin Glover, Carla Hassel, Pamela Gustavson Johnson, Pat Morris, Mary Schafer, Nancy Smeltzer, Fran Soika, Judy Howard of Buckboard Antiques and Quilts, Oklahoma City, Oklahoma; Jean Lyle of C & L Enterprises, Quincy, Illinois; Phyllis Nye of Calico 'N Things, Marquette, Michigan; Kathy and Ron Hind of Hickory Hill Antiques, Redmond, Washington; Susan Parrett and Rod Lich of Folkways, Georgetown, Indiana; Tracy Jamar of Jamar Textile Restoration Studio, New York City; Living History Farms Museum, Urbandale, Iowa; John Sauls' Antiques, Tyler, Texas; Smithsonian Institution, Washington, D.C.; Spencer Museum of Art at the University of Kansas, Lawrence Kansas; The Wild Goose Chase Quilt Gallery of Evanston, Illinois; and all of the quilters and collectors who are included in this book.

Because this book is based upon photographic reproductions, of both antique and contemporary quilts, I should like to thank the following photographers for working with me to make the best possible photographs available: Schecter Lee Studios, New York City; Gilstrap Photography, Hurst, Texas; Award Photography, Irving, Texas; and Jerry Darvin Photography, Brooklyn, New York. Special thanks also to my friend and photographer Ed Rousseau of Rousseau Studio, Flint, Michigan, for devoting a day off to the book, and to Artsource Gallery in Flint for providing the studio space in which to shoot. Last but not least, big hugs go to my husband, Dean, for being my "photographer on call" for the duration of the book.

Finally, I should like to express sincere appreciation to my proofreader, Sandra Rundell of Flushing, Michigan, for wielding her red pencil with great skill, and to Cyril I. Nelson, my editor at Dutton, for making this book possible.

CONTENTS

A New Look for an Old Craft

In days gone by, a large portion of the quilts made were utility quilts serving a specific function: keeping people warm. Sometimes piled five and six layers high on a bed, quilts were often the only means of staying warm on a cold winter night. When a quilt was too old or tattered to be used as a covering, it was often recycled. Old quilts were used as coverings for animals in the barn, were hung across a doorway to stop drafts from entering a room, stacked and used as an additional mattress, wrapped around precious furniture when it was moved from one house to another, or were placed inside a new quilt top and the backing when times were hard and cotton was scarce. Because there was always something they could be used for, quilts were seldom tossed away.

When the first group of settlers arrived, patchwork was introduced into the New World. Patchwork patterns that had been in use for several hundred years, passed down from one generation to another, were brought over from Europe and England. Each new generation of quilters altered the look of the designs by changing the color, size, layout, and border treatment, but basic patterns remained the same.

Beginning in the late 1800s, newspapers often supplied women with printed patterns on a regular basis, and as the years passed, magazines gradually picked up on the importance of needlework in women's lives. *The Progressive Farmer, Hearth and Home, Ladies Art Company, The Kansas City Star, Needlecraft Magazine,* and *Capper's Weekly Quilt Block Service* all became popular sources for patchwork and quilting patterns.

Sewing skills were a part of every girl's education, which began at the early age of three or four. Youngsters, instructed by their mothers, older sisters, aunts, and other family members, were taught how to do cross-stitch, embroidery, needlepoint, and other fancywork. During quilting bees children were kept busy threading needles for the women at the quilt frame. As children grew older, they were shown how to piece simple blocks like the Four Patch and Nine Patch, turning out tiny doll quilts and crib quilts. A baker's dozen of quilts was often the only dowry a girl had when she married, and work began on these quilts as girls approached their teens.

Because of the monetary restrictions on many families, women had no alternative but to make use of what was available to them. They took pride in transforming something as ragged as an old apron into part of a beautifully appliquéd or pieced quilt. Tender care was taken to be as accurate as possible in the planning and piecing of each quilt, as the final product would be a testimony to the woman who made it.

Fabrics were taken from children's clothing, men's tattered shirts, usable areas from well-worn aprons, and other garments. These scraps were then used in quilts rather than being wasted. Every inch of cloth was saved in

1. Pine Tree, full size, collection of Robert and Nancy Peters, Cedar Falls, Iowa. This delightful Pine Tree quilt was given a sneak preview in the December 1982 issue of *Country Living Magazine*, where only a corner of the quilt was visible as it covered a bed. The scrap quilt features hand-pieced blocks measuring 11″ square and alternating with plain white blocks. Photograph by E. Rousseau, Flushing, Michigan.

2. *Reflections on Arnheim*, 83″ x 83″, copyright 1979 by Pamela Gustavson Johnson, Kansas City, Missouri. Based on the traditional Pinwheel Star pattern. Photograph by Schecter Lee.

a scrap bag to be used at some point in time in a special quilt. Many times, gathered scraps would suggest a particular pattern to the quilter. Men's heavy trousers and other equally thick fabrics were good possibilities for quilts that needed little or no hand quilting, such as in a Log Cabin. Delicate pastel colors were reserved for baby or bridal quilts. Purchasing fabric for the sole purpose of making a quilt was uncommon, and such a purchase was saved for the creation of a very special quilt.

During the last two decades the changes in quilting have been enormous. Fabrics such as velvet, satin, silk, lamé, and other fabrics seldom seen in quilts in the mid-1900s are being used more often. The use of subtle gradations of color is becoming more frequent as quilters hand-dye their own fabrics, and a trend toward originality of design is growing steadily. New techniques and tools created to simplify the process of quiltmaking are springing up in quilt shops and shows around the country, and the number of quilt instructors seems to grow daily.

No longer are quilts a necessity for warmth. Central heating and solar heating have made excessive amounts of bedding unnecessary, and commercially made comforters and electric blankets have taken the place of quilts in most homes. Today, quilts are sometimes used on beds but for an entirely different reason: decoration. Quilts are purchased as collectible items at high prices, and for some individuals they serve as status symbols in their homes. As if these changes weren't enough, quilts have moved from bed to wall, and are frequently found on exhibit in prominent art galleries.

Because of the intense interest in quiltmaking today, quilting has become a thriving business. There are people who do nothing but travel around the country lecturing on and teaching quilting at seminars and for nonprofit organizations set up for the sole benefit of quilters. Many, many publishers—both large and small—have brought out hundreds of quilting books and patterns. Companies have been formed to promote quilters, exhibits at shopping malls, and teachers. Galleries dealing primarily in quilts have been established, and quilting has even become computerized with the introduction of software intended to simplify the design process.

Through the years, quilts have gradually changed in appearance. There are many names assigned to the various styles and sizes of quilts being made today. First, there is the *art quilt*, a general term used to describe modern fabric paintings; *wall quilt*, which loosely refers to any quilt made to hang on a wall, not to cover a bed; and *miniature quilts*, tiny half-pint versions of full-size quilts. Some of the styles that have frequently been made during the 1970s and 1980s are *shadow quilts*, white quilts that use a lightweight batiste fabric to cover a collage of colored fabric or yarn; *mandalas*, quilts based on divided circles; and *whole-cloth quilts*, quilts made of one-color fabric, in which the design has been quilted rather than pieced or appliquéd. The technique is similar to that used during the early 1800s, but using new shapes and quilt motifs. *Stained-glass quilts* resemble stained-glass windows, with narrow strips of black fabric separating bright solid colors. The term *Hawaiian quilting* encompasses all two-tone quilts in which the design is cut from a single piece of fabric that has been folded like a snowflake. *Medallion quilts*, popular in England during the late 1700s and the first half of the 1800s, were recently brought back into vogue by Jinny Beyer. Medallion quilts have a center design around which all other portions of the quilt revolve. Many of the styles mentioned above can be combined into a single quilt. It is entirely possible to create a miniature whole-cloth mandala wall quilt or an abstract stained-glass medallion. Most types of quilts can be made in any number of different techniques: appliqué, piecing, reverse appliqué, Seminole stripping, strip piecing, candlewicking, trapunto, and so forth. It's enough to make any beginner's head spin!

Quilts of the 1980s are certainly a mixed breed. Artists and quiltmakers experimenting in fiber art are creating new and unusual quilts using paints, rhinestones, glitter, paper, and photographic methods of imprinting images on fabric.

Contemporary Quilts from Traditional Designs takes a comparative look at the physical changes in the art of quilting through the years. While the overall appearance of quilts has changed, many contemporary quiltmakers keep coming back to traditional patterns. Just as a quiltmaker in the late 1800s might have altered a pattern to fit her needs, so are today's quilters making their own necessary changes. The artists represented in this book have not only graciously allowed the publication of their work, but also share their feelings on the history of quilting, the direction in which it is going, and their viewpoints on several quilt-related topics.

3. Postage Stamp, 70″ x 50″, c. 1910. Collection of Jean Teal, Farmhouse Fabrics, Oconomowoc, Wisconsin. Photograph by E. Rousseau.

POSTAGE STAMP: TRADITIONAL

Postage Stamp quilts represent the very heart of quiltmaking: the art of making something out of nothing. In the late 1700s and early 1800s, women used every scrap of fabric available, from worn clothing to flour sacks. No piece of fabric was too small to discard, as shown by the many Postage Stamp quilts that are still in existence.

The name, Postage Stamp, precisely describes the essence of the pattern, for the size of the individual squares is roughly the size of a postage stamp. Although the exact dimensions of the square vary from quilt to quilt, most examples contain squares that average an inch in width.

The quiltmaker of this 1910 Postage Stamp is unknown, but the information available indicates she lived in Sun Prairie, Wisconsin. The quilt is one of a matching pair made by a mother-and-daughter team.

It is interesting to observe the placement of fabric scraps in the quilt. On the lower portion of the quilt, eight gold squares have been randomly placed, the only solid-color fabric used. Across the top third of the quilt, a pink print has been used in abundance. Other fabrics are placed in groupings, suggesting that this quilt was made as fabrics could be found. Plaids, stripes, and other men's shirting fabrics are the major materials used. A small addition of a very delicate, shimmery brown print may be left over from a good dress the quilter may have made.

A new binding has replaced the old one, but the quilt remains in good condition even though it shows proof of use and years of love.

4. *October Landscape*, 95″ x 85″, made by Susan Locher, Tallmadge, Ohio. Collection of Bob Kohler, Kettering, Ohio. Photograph by Alan McFarland.

POSTAGE STAMP: CONTEMPORARY

Many of the Postage Stamp quilts made by quilters today are pictorially designed, either by following a charted needlepoint pattern or by graphing out an original design. Each square on the graph is usually equal to one square on the quilt, although the size of the squares can vary from a quarter inch to two inches.

Susan Locher, a quilter from Tallmadge, Ohio, has used one-inch squares in her *October Landscape,* an abstract pictorial symbolizing the beauty of the color changes in autumn. Susan has handled the color in her quilt with the skill of a painter applying a brush to canvas. At the same time she pays homage to quilters of the past.

SUSAN LOCHER: "I had been reading a book about some quilters in Texas who told of how they used every little inch of fabric in their quilts, and got to thinking that this is basically what a quilt is meant to be, so I decided to do something using scraps. It was October at the time and the idea just sort of evolved. Most of the fabrics are cotton and polyester blend with some pieces of satin and taffeta included to give the effect of light shining on the leaves. I did make it with scraps, only having to purchase the extra materials needed for the border.

"There are a lot more people making 'designer' quilts or original designs now than there were in the past, but in many ways I don't think quilting has changed that much over the years. There seems to be a lot of interest among younger people, while I remember when I was a teenager we thought of quilting as a nice thing, but certainly nothing we wanted to do. I feel there is a lot more emphasis on color and blending the materials now than there used to be. Fewer of us actually make scrap quilts using leftover materials than quilters of the past."

October Landscape was exhibited at the Firelands Association for Visual Arts (FAVA) gallery Design '85 Exhibit of Functional Art, Oberlin, Ohio, where it shared the judges' Artist Award with Susan's *Nova,* shown on page 21.

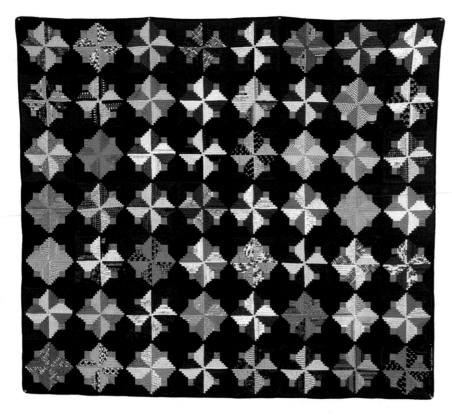

5. Log Cabin, 66″ x 74″, c. 1890, maker unknown. Collection of N. Dean and Caron L. Mosey, Flushing, Michigan. Photograph by E. Rousseau.

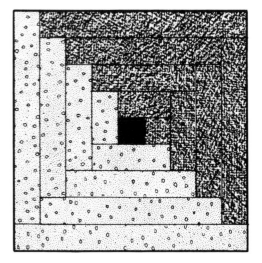

LOG CABIN: TRADITIONAL

The Log Cabin block is one of the best known of all traditional quilting patterns. Many quilters refer to this design as a technique rather than a pattern, as the variations in size, shape, and color are seemingly endless. Courthouse Steps, Pineapple, Straight Furrow, Barn Raising, Capital Steps, Light and Dark, and Zigzag are some of the many designs that can be made in the Log Cabin style.

A traditional square Log Cabin block begins with a "chimney" in the center. The name for this small center square harks back to the days of log cabins when the fireplace (often located in the center of the house) served as the sole source of heat. The "chimney" in a Log Cabin block is often made of a red or black fabric, which further emphasizes the origins of the design. This small square is surrounded by several rows of rectangular strips placed in a clockwise manner, simulating the layering of timbers in a log cabin. As each round of four strips is added, the block increases in size. There is no set rule for the size of the block or the number of pieces used in it. As a true scrap quilt with an endless assortment of fabrics, or as a two-tone quilt, the Log Cabin continues to be just as popular today as it was in the 1800s.

The antique Log Cabin shown here is made in the Light and Dark pattern. The mixture of various fabrics such as velvet, satin, taffeta, and ribbon forms a pleasing sense of texture. This mixture, combined with the contrast of vivid colors and solid black, is a visual delight. This quilt is unusual in that the quilting is visible on the back of the quilt but does not continue through to the front. It is my guess that the Log Cabin quilt top was sewn on top of a badly worn quilt.

6. *Muplex*, 45″ x 45″, copyright 1985 by Mary Jo Dalrymple, Little Rock, Arkansas. Collection of the artist. Photograph by Bill Parsons.

LOG CABIN: CONTEMPORARY

Because of the flexibility of the Log Cabin technique, it can be used in hundreds of different ways. Whether the blocks are square, triangular, or hexagonal, the process of creating additional rows of strips leaves much room for the quilter to expand on tradition.

Mary Jo Dalrymple of Little Rock, Arkansas, has made many beautiful wall quilts with the Log Cabin technique. Her quilt *Muplex,* shown here, is a fine example of her ability to spice up tradition.

MARY JO DALRYMPLE: "Modernizing was not a conscious effort. I recognized an elegant arrangement of shapes as being compatible with my ideas at the time. As quilters, we can work through a traditional design and say something very personal and important. People have worked through the human figure forever, and still it usually appears in the same traditional shape; i.e., two arms, two legs, one head—the same old shape, but forever new, always expressive in the right hands.

"In thinking about my process in creating quilts, I'm reminded of what Pooh Bear said... 'the more I looked for it, the more it wasn't there.' Most of my designing is done in my mind. There is always a simmering of thoughts, colors, feelings, shapes, etc. There is a certain time when everything reaches a level of vitality and starts to solidify in a certain direction. That is when I go to my materials. The big task, of course, is to change what the mind knows into what the eye can see."

Muplex is certainly an exciting change from the familiar Log Cabin style. While the "chimney" remains, the block has taken on an entirely new look. Sharply contrasting colors blended with large open spaces work together to create a three-dimensional appearance. Mary Jo's tasteful addition of a small amount of reds, oranges, and yellows adds just the right sprinkling of warmth to the cool tones of her quilt, revealing her artistic flair and proficiency as a contemporary quiltmaker.

7. Pine Tree, 69″ x 88″, c. 1875. Quilt and photograph courtesy Susan Parrett and Rod Lich of Folkways, Georgetown, Indiana.

PINE TREE: TRADITIONAL

Sometimes called the Tree of Life, the Pine Tree pattern is one that has been altered by virtually every quilter who has attempted to make it. Changes in the size and shape of the trunk, the placing of a "base" at the bottom of the trunk, and the number of rows of "foliage" in the tree are all variables that can be modified. Pieced with small triangles set upon a trunk, the Pine Tree is normally placed in a diagonal setting and contains large open areas that are excellent for showing off fancy quilting motifs and tiny stitches.

The Pine Tree shown here is believed to have been made around 1875 in southern Indiana. Christmas reds and greens give a holiday appearance to this elaborately stitched treasure. Large feather wreaths, cross-hatching, and a double binding of red and green reveal the talents of an experienced hand.

A pattern for a basic Pine Tree block may be found on page 89.

8. *From the Woods to the Water*, 82″ x 82″, copyright 1983 by Caron L. Mosey. Collection of Robert and Betty Covert, Flushing, Michigan. Photograph by E. Rousseau.

PINE TREE: CONTEMPORARY

From the Woods to the Water was created by combining two traditional patterns to symbolize my parents' retirement move from a house in the woods to a home on Lake Michigan. The Pine Tree block, radiating out to each of the four corners of the quilt, has long been a symbol of the woodlands, and it served as the perfect reminder of some twenty-five years that they spent surrounded by trees. The Mariner's Compass in the center of the quilt represents the water and the many seaworthy vessels that pass by the channel at Charlevoix, Michigan.

The flexibility of the width and length of the "tree trunk" made the pattern easily adaptable for use as a suitable frame for the Mariner's Compass. The "trunk" of each tree is quilted every quarter inch, with the open areas containing a quilted ship's wheel motif of an original design. Fabrics of 100 percent cotton in prints and solids have been used in combination with a polyester batting to measure 82 inches square.

9. Attic Windows, 15″ x 13½″, made in 1986 by the author. Photograph by Charles Scroggins.

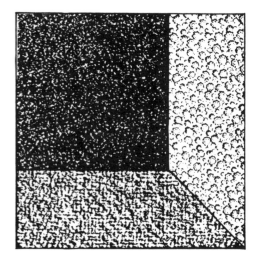

ATTIC WINDOWS: TRADITIONAL

As a full-size quilt or a small doll quilt, the Attic Windows pattern is simple and quick to piece for even the beginning quiltmaker. Using a square of any size as a starting point, strips of fabric are added to two sides and mitered to create a three-dimensional effect resembling a window. Many antique quilts found in this pattern have been made of beautiful silks, velvets, and other delicate fabrics. Because of the few pattern pieces required, Attic Windows is a good pattern to choose for utilizing "better" fabrics to their best advantage.

The small doll quilt shown here was made in colors similar to those used in antique Amish quilts. Straight lines forming an X have been quilted in each of the black squares, and a continuous line of quilting follows the rectangular shape of the outermost border. Because of the small size of the quilt and the simplicity of the piecing, this is a perfect quilt for a weekend project for quilters of all levels.

Patterns with which to make an Attic Windows block of this small two-inch-square size plus a larger size can be found on page 92.

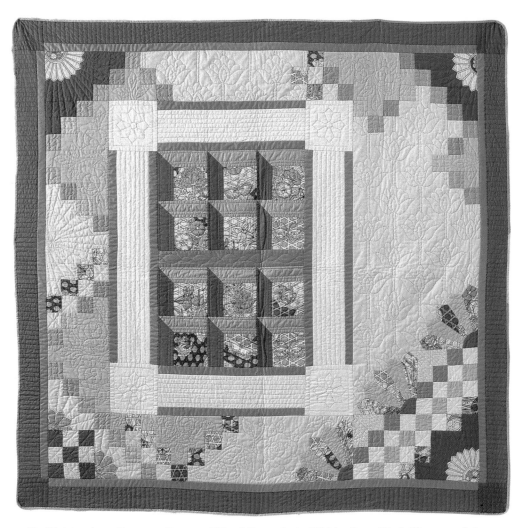

10. *Waiting for a Summer Breeze*, 60″ x 64″, made in 1984 by Jean Eitel. Photograph by Schecter Lee.

ATTIC WINDOWS: CONTEMPORARY

Waiting for a Summer Breeze, created by Jean Eitel in 1984, developed as the result of a dream. Living in North Palm Beach, Florida, the artist found it hard to adjust to the intense heat and humidity that comes with summer there. After spending one July night suspended between hazy consciousness and sleep and trying to stay cool, Jean woke thinking about the ceiling fans stirring the air and longed for a cool summer breeze to blow through her window.

Jean's quilt is alive with many traditional quilting patterns that symbolize her dream: Attic Windows, Grandmother's Fan, Nine Patch, and One Patch. The focal point of the quilt, the central Attic Windows section, figuratively allows the heat to escape from and the cool air to enter the room. An array of pastel and cool colors are contained within the dark borders of the quilt. Exquisite floral designs serve as delicate quilting motifs to soften the straight lines of the pattern.

Currently the editor of *Quilt Magazine,* Jean is also the author of *Creative Quiltmaking in the Mandala Tradition,* published by Chilton Books.

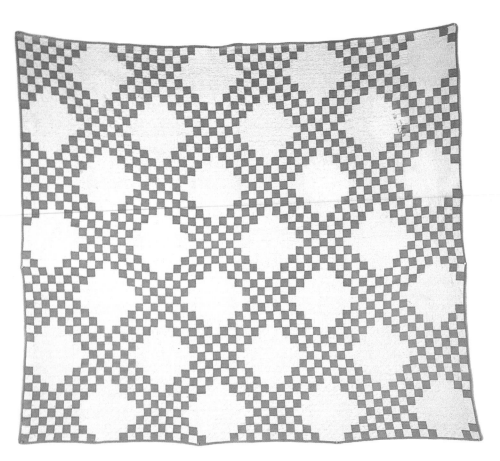

11. Triple Irish Chain, 69″ x 80″, c. 1880. Quilt courtesy Jean Lyle, C & L Enterprises, Quincy, Illinois. Photograph by E. Rousseau.

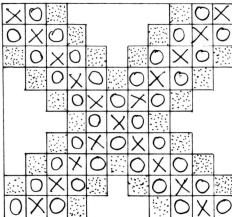

TRIPLE IRISH CHAIN: TRADITIONAL

Triple Irish Chain, a simple two-tone pattern based on a square, is made elegant by the use of tastefully chosen fabrics and intricate quilting motifs. While most of our ancestors tediously hand-pieced each square together, quiltmakers today often complete a quilt top in this pattern with a rapidity made possible by strip-piecing techniques.

This light brown and white quilt, owned by Jean Lyle of Illinois, was made in Perry, Missouri, in the late 1800s.

The soft pastel brown is an unusual color not often seen in Irish Chain quilts; stronger and brighter colors are usually used to achieve a sharp contrast with the white background. Double and triple rows of straight quilting run across the patterned top, and cotton seeds are visible through the lining of the quilt, possibly revealing a batting that was hand-carded by the maker. A quarter-inch binding of the original brown material remains in excellent condition despite the age of the quilt.

12. *Triple Irish Chain,* 42″ x 42″, made in 1983 by Margery Cosgrove. Photograph by Schecter Lee.

TRIPLE IRISH CHAIN: CONTEMPORARY

The traditional version of the Triple Irish Chain pattern contains wide areas of plain fabric that are usually filled with an intricate quilting motif. After hours of playing with the pattern, Margery Cosgrove altered this portion of the design in her contemporary Triple Irish Chain. "The white area in the Irish Chain dominated the design; so to redirect the focus, I added a new 'flower' in each square." The result is a charming wall hanging which, when studied, appears to have four arrows pointing toward each of the four corners.

MARGERY COSGROVE: "Color and light are very important elements in my work. [In quilts today,] individuality and design seem to be stressed very heavily. The quilt as our heritage, our roots, is being reworked in the contemporary quilt through our ingenuity and resourcefulness. Good quiltmaking will always be good workmanship, but I do feel that the 'perfect' quilt is rather sterile and lifeless. The lovely old quilts have a sense of humor with their little endearing 'mistakes.' I hope our new quilts will keep these elements with the human factor made visible."

Triple Irish Chain is often made of matching fabrics, but Margery's skillful use of scrap-bag fabrics adds a warm homespun touch to an otherwise contemporary quilt. As an artist, Margery has won awards in several different mediums, including painting, weaving, clothing design, and now quiltmaking. She has worked as a free-lance designer for Intermedia and Procter & Gamble, and has been published in Bucky King's *Ecclesiastical Crafts* and the *Goodfellow Catalog of Wonderful Things.*

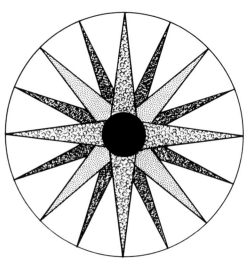

13. Mariner's Compass, 84″ x 84″, maker unknown, c. 1870. Joyce Aufderheide Collection. Photograph by E. Rousseau.

MARINER'S COMPASS: TRADITIONAL

The Mariner's Compass, a pattern definitely reserved for advanced quiltmakers, has its roots in the early navigation maps used by seamen years ago. The compass design, although remaining technically accurate, was drawn in many variations by cartographers. From plain arrows to fancy circular designs, the compass has been made with as few as four directional points to as many as thirty-two or more.

This red and green Mariner's Compass quilt, owned by Joyce Aufderheide of New Ulm, Minnesota, was made in the 1870s in Cleveland, Minnesota. The compass circles

measure 17 inches across the center and are set into a 20½-inch square. Appliqúes of leaves and buds enliven each intersection and form a beautifully delicate border. A thin red and white sawtooth border meets with the less-than-quarter-inch binding. Close crosshatched quilting covers the open areas between the blocks, and diagonal quilting lines fill in the border areas nicely. This well-preserved treasure serves as a perfect example of accurate piecing in an otherwise difficult pattern.

For quilters who appreciate a real challenge, a pattern for a Mariner's Compass block can be found on page 96.

14. *Cathedral Window*, 90″ x 72″, copyright 1984 by Caryl Bryer Fallert. Photograph by E. Rousseau.

MARINER'S COMPASS: CONTEMPORARY

Caryl Bryer Fallert of Oswego, Illinois, has taken liberties with the large open spaces within the points of the traditional Mariner's Compass.

CARYL BRYER FALLERT: "I wanted my design to be totally original. The compass format appealed to me and seemed as if it would be a challenge to execute, using both straight and curved lines. It also provided a good outline for a large-format design that could fill the center of a quilt, while allowing room to play with patterns within its design elements."

Cathedral Window, the title of her contemporary Mariner's Compass, is made of cotton and acetate velvets and men's tie fabrics. Her choice of fabrics was intentional: "I wanted to give the feeling of a rose window in a Gothic cathedral. Fabrics were chosen for their richness and tactile qualities."

The backing of the quilt is shiny raspberry-colored acetate satin. Although most antique quilts are made of cotton and wool fabrics, Caryl feels that "the best fabric is the one that best expresses what the artist wants to communicate."

In thinking over the changes in quilting over the years, Caryl feels that "quilting has progressed from a necessary part of everyday life to a leisure-time activity. Because of this, modern quiltmakers can leave the bed format and pursue the manipulation of fabric as an art form with no function other than adding beauty to people's lives."

In 1981, after fifteen years as a painter, Caryl transferred her love of color and texture to the quilt medium. She studied art at Illinois State University, University of Wisconsin, College of DuPage, and Wheaton College, where she received her B.A. in 1969. Her work has been included in many exhibitions across the country, and in April 1986 she visited the Peoples Republic of China as part of a citizen-ambassador program, giving a presentation about her work and quiltmaking in the United States.

15

15. Jacob's Ladder, 90″ x 79″, c. 1860, maker unknown. Quilt courtesy Phyllis Nye, Calico 'N Things, Marquette, Michigan. Photograph by Rousseau Studio, Flint, Michigan.

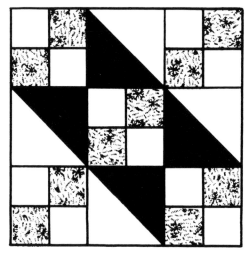

JACOB'S LADDER: TRADITIONAL

Jacob's Ladder is a fairly simple pattern that has been popular for many generations. A number of variations of the pattern have evolved over the years, but the version shown here is the most widely known of all.

The large triangles that point toward the center of each block are usually made of the same fabric, usually in a dark color, to give a feeling of motion to the quilt. In this piece, owned by Phyllis Nye of Calico 'N Things, these triangles have been made of both printed and solid fabrics. Yellow squares set between the red sashing strips

tie the block together and give a uniformity to this essentially scrap-bag quilt.

The quilt top shown here (not including the two brown borders) dates back to the late 1800s to early 1900s. New fabric has been added to the outer edges of the top to enlarge and strengthen it, and it has been put together with a polyester batting and new print lining.

A basic Jacob's Ladder pattern can be found on page 93.

(16a, left). *Jacob's Ladder Number 1 Concave*, 26″ x 26″, made in 1986 by Barbara Caron. (16b, right). *Jacob's Ladder Number 2 Convex*, 26″ x 26″, made in 1986 by Barbara Caron. Photographs by Schecter Lee.

JACOB'S LADDER: CONTEMPORARY

Quilter and teacher Barbara Caron, of St. Paul, Minnesota, has experimented with the Jacob's Ladder block, creating two variations on a theme: concave curves in her first quilt, and convex curves in her second. When asked about her attempts to "modernize" this traditional pattern, she offered these reasons.

BARBARA CARON: "First I like the traditional Jacob's Ladder block because it is asymmetrical and offers some interesting possibilities for use of value and setting. At the same time, I like my work to have an interesting new look. I also wanted to do a series of wall quilts based on a single block and setting. By using the curved two-patch system, I was able to accomplish these goals. As I began cutting patches and making

final decisions, I decided that the small pieces would be identical in use of fabric and setting and that only the variation of the curve (concave or convex) would be different. I have also made a traditional piece consisting of four nine-inch blocks rotated around a center point and bordered. The result of the three wall hangings together is called a 'triptych.'"

Barb's Jacob's Ladder wall hangings are made of 100 percent cotton fabrics, as are all her quilts. Her clever use of the curved two-patch system (developed by Joyce Schlotzhauer) to modify triangular shapes can be applied to other traditional quilt patterns as well, and can provide a whole new spectrum of design possibilities.

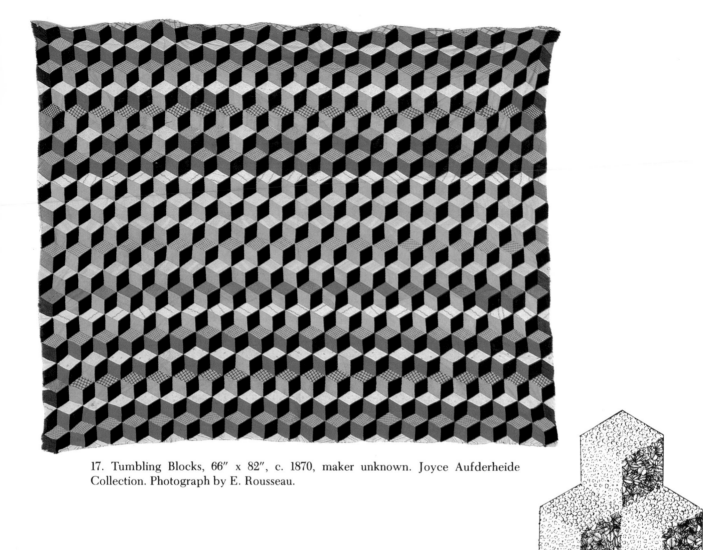

17. Tumbling Blocks, 66″ x 82″, c. 1870, maker unknown. Joyce Aufderheide Collection. Photograph by E. Rousseau.

TUMBLING BLOCKS: TRADITIONAL

Sometimes also called Baby Blocks or Children's Blocks, this quilt is made using one major template, a diamond. The shading of fabrics, if done carefully, will give a three-dimensional effect resembling a stack of baby's blocks.

The quilt top shown here, made in the 1870s, was hand-pieced in Ohio and is an outstanding example of optical illusion. Depending on the way you look at the quilt, boxes, stars, or the black fabrics come forward as being the dominant shape or color. From the collection of Joyce Aufderheide, this quilt top was enclosed with another quilt she purchased in the 1960s, a pleasant bonus for any avid collector.

The Tumbling Blocks pattern is common in antique Amish quilts, where three solid shades of traditional Amish colors work together to produce a very simple but elegant geometric statement. Another example of a Tumbling Blocks quilt can be found on page 71.

The basic pattern for Tumbling Blocks is given on page 80.

18. *Chimera*, 105½″ x 91″, made in 1985 by Marlene Andrey. Photograph by E. Rousseau.

TUMBLING BLOCKS: CONTEMPORARY

Chimera, created by Marlene Andrey, was made as an experiment following the advice in Jeff Gutcheon's book *Diamond Patchwork*. The impetus behind this large quilt was an advertisement for floor tiles! By drafting a diamond version of the pattern in the tile, Marlene was able to come up with a design that closely resembles the traditional Tumbling Blocks pattern. *Chimera* includes an appealing array of shimmery acetate, acetate blends, chintz, and cotton-polyester-blend fabrics, proof that Marlene does not feel restricted to 100 percent cotton fabric as many traditional quiltmakers do.

Marlene took her first quilting class in 1978, and since then she has entered her quilts in several local shows, picking up several awards in the process. *Chimera* was accepted and exhibited at the American Quilter's Society Second Annual Show (1986) in Paducah, Kentucky. This

was the first "long-distance" trip for any Andrey creation. Her willingness to "play" with the various elements of quiltmaking has helped her improve in technique and workmanship since her first quilt was completed.

MARLENE ANDREY: "It is very hard for me to describe how I construct a quilt because there is no method to my madness. I just 'kinda do it!' I start off with an idea and play around with it until I come up with something. Some things work and some don't. I try to work out most of the details on paper before I go to the fabric, but as I work, I get ideas and change my mind. Even when I'm into the fabric, I can usually change things around. Sometimes this can get rather costly. Usually, the quilt I end up with is not like the initial idea."

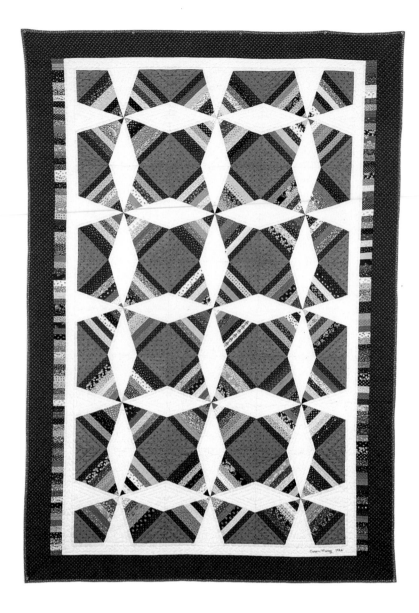

19. Spider's Web, 83″ x 58½″, made in 1986 by the author and quilted by an Amish friend in Shipshewana, Indiana. Photograph by E. Rousseau.

SPIDER'S WEB: TRADITIONAL

The Spider's Web patchwork pattern has often been confused with the Spider's Web quilting motif. Although they share the same name, each is a separate technique. The pattern shown in the diagram above and in the quilt illustrated is a pieced pattern utilizing a strip-piecing method of assembly. Used in the 1800s in scrap quilts, this pattern is based upon the outline of a simply woven spider's web, and several variations of the pattern have been used. This odd-sized cover was made to keep my family warm while they pursue their favorite indoor hobby: watching TV.

Using a rotary cutter, strips of fabric from my scrap bag were cut in a short time and then sewn together, forming random rows of color. A light chocolate-brown print forms a square where each block is joined to another, and the slate-blue print sprinkled throughout the quilt has been used as a border to give the quilt a "country" appearance.

The large white areas that appear as diamonds are formed by the assembly of the blocks. In many antique quilts this area is also made of strips of fabric, tightening up the overall appearance of the quilt. Either way, the pattern provides a charming outline for a beautiful scrap quilt.

20. *Nova*, 95″ x 85″, made in 1984 by Susan Locher. Photograph by Alan McFarland.

SPIDER'S WEB: CONTEMPORARY

Susan Locher of Tallmadge, Ohio, did not set out to make a contemporary version of the traditional Spider's Web pattern; it happened quite by mistake. "I completely designed this quilt and made it, only to be informed that there is an old pattern called a Spider's Web which is very similar."

The quilt, titled *Nova*, is made of bands of black satin, bright colored satin, grosgrain and velvet ribbon, and was made in eight sections. *Nova* is one of a series of quilts using black as a background to enhance the vitality of the colors used in each quilt. *Nova*, which means an exploding star, captures the forceful effect the warm colors have when blended with the shimmery fabric.

Nova was exhibited at the Firelands Association for Visual Arts (FAVA) gallery in Oberlin, Ohio, in the spring of 1985 where it earned an Artist Award. It was also shown at the Canton Art Institute in the "All Ohio 1986" exhibition.

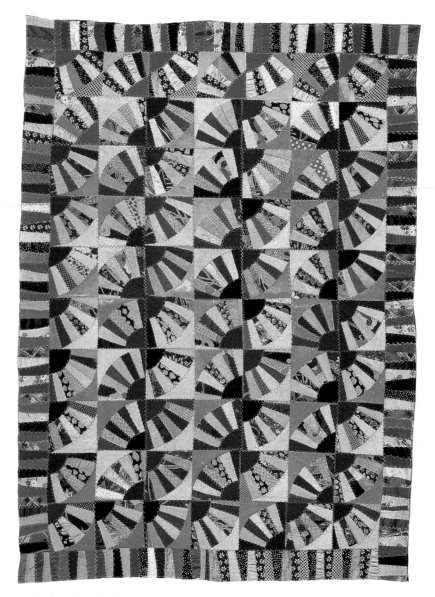

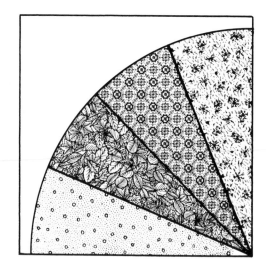

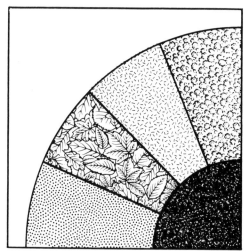

21. Grandmother's Fan, 75″ x 54″, c. 1880. Collection of Madeleine Appell, Brooklyn, New York. Photograph by Jerry Darvin Photography, Brooklyn, New York.

GRANDMOTHER'S FAN: TRADITIONAL

Grandmother's Fan is a pattern that lends itself to fancy lace, embroidery, and elegant fabrics not normally associated with pieced quilts. The block can be appliquéd or pieced, although it is usually made by using a combination of the two techniques. In the latter method, the main segments of the block are pieced together and then appliquéd to a square background fabric, generally of a lighter color.

Madeleine Appell of Brooklyn, New York, purchased this exquisite Grandmother's Fan in 1980 at the Brooklyn Historical Society Shop in Brooklyn, New York. Made by an unknown quilter, this piece is in the style of the Crazy Quilts of the late 1800s. A variety of embroidery stitches covers each seam and adds interest to the quilt. Short strips of fabric have been sewn together into long rows that form the border, and each is outlined with a thread of contrasting color.

A basic pattern for the Grandmother's Fan can be found on page 81.

22. *Tents of Armageddon*, 64½″ x 67″, made in 1980 by Virginia Randles, Athens, Ohio. Photograph courtesy the artist.

GRANDMOTHER'S FAN: CONTEMPORARY

Based on the Grandmother's Fan pattern, *Tents of Armageddon* by Virginia Randles uses graduated shades of blue. Working from the inside with light shades, the blues become darker toward the outer borders. As the fan blocks move closer to the edges of the quilt, they are spaced farther apart.

The traditional version of Grandmother's Fan is divided into more sections per block than those found in *Tents of Armageddon*; however, a study of antique Fan quilts shows considerable flexibility in the number of divisions found in each quilt. The fan in each block of *Tents of Armageddon* is divided into two parts, with the left section being a shade darker than the right. The curved sections of the quilt contain minimal quilting, perhaps in an attempt to make them stand out. The black background, however, is heavily quilted with cross-hatching. A border of deep blue against the jet-black fabric is reminiscent of the borders in many old Amish quilts.

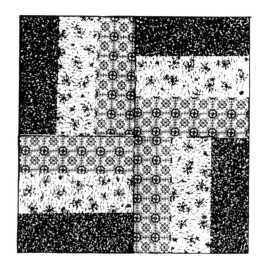

23. Rail Fence, 60″ x 44″, made in 1986 by the author. Photograph by E. Rousseau.

RAIL FENCE: TRADITIONAL

The Rail Fence is a simple pattern that any beginner can easily learn. As seen here, each block is divided into four sections, and each section contains three strips of fabric. In this quilt, the resulting design is known as the Spirit of St. Louis. It is possible to adjust the number of strips in each section, thus changing the look of the block and overall design. If more strips are used, the "crosses" (seen in the blue fabric here) are not visible and the pattern resembles a pieced checkerboard.

This quilt, made in 1986 to be a "snuggle-under-to-watch-TV" quilt for my five-year-old son, uses three contrasting colors. Curved arches, called "fan quilting," have been stitched over the pattern, with diagonal quilting used throughout the border, making this a fast quilt to stitch. Additional information on fan quilting can be found in an article by Joe Cunningham on page 50 of the November 1986 issue of *Lady's Circle Patchwork Quilts.*

The pattern for the Rail Fence block is on page 95.

24. *Sailor's Delight*, 66″ x 66″, copyright 1984 by Flavin Glover. Photograph by Glenn R. Glover.

RAIL FENCE: CONTEMPORARY

It is hard to believe that the pattern used to design *Sailor's Delight* is the same one that was used to make the simple quilt on page 24. Flavin Glover, of Auburn, Alabama, has carefully selected varying shades of orange and blue fabrics to create this marvelous fabric painting inspired by the old saying "Red sky at night, sailor's delight."

Because of the similarity in texture and closely calibrated coloring of the fabrics, the strong lines of the block have all but disappeared and merge together in this piece to create a solid mass of color. At first glance, the quilt seems to be constructed from random bits of fabric, as in a scrap quilt. However, a closer look reveals the handiwork of a very talented artist. Notice how the water seems to reflect the sky and how the sun's circle is mirrored in the water.

Most of Flavin's quilts are based to some degree on traditional patterns because they are "familiar and handy." Even though she works within a specific grid system that she has ruled on graph paper, she freely modifies the old to achieve the new. Flavin Glover is a freelance designer whose work has been published regularly in *Better Homes and Gardens*, *Quilter's Newsletter Magazine*, *Quilt Magazine*, and *The Quilt: New Directions for an American Tradition*. Her quilts are included in several private and public collections, including the Alabama State 4-H Conference Center in Columbiana, Alabama, and the State Office Building in Montgomery, Alabama.

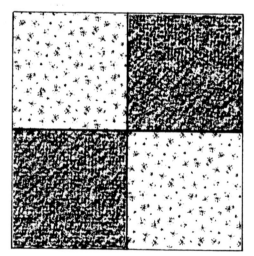

25. Double Four Patch, 78″ x 70″, c. 1900, from Missouri. Quilt courtesy Jean Lyle, C & L Enterprises, Quincy, Illinois. Photograph by E. Rousseau.

FOUR PATCH: TRADITIONAL

Four Patch is a pattern that many beginning quiltmakers of all ages use to learn the basics of patchwork. Its straight lines and only one intersection where points must meet make it a fast and versatile pattern. When placed in a setting with alternating solid blocks, large open areas provide space for either elaborate quilting motifs or the straight quilting lines that have been used in this piece.

The quilt shown here has Double Four Patch blocks alternating with white blocks. Cheerful yellow fabric has

been used in each pieced block and also for the binding to brighten up the darker fabrics.

Probably made as a quilt to be used rather than saved for "good," this Four Patch has held up well through the years. The quilt top was probably made around the turn of the century and was quilted in the 1930s. Discovered in a Perry, Missouri, antiques shop, this quilt is a fine cheery addition to any collection, and it well represents the foundations of the craft.

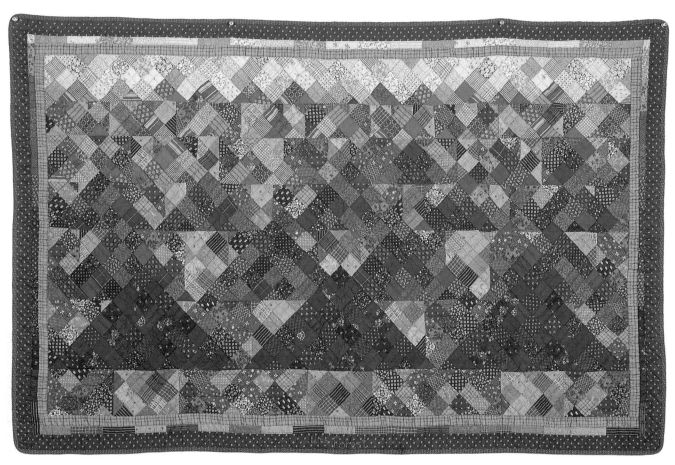

26. *Fourth Forest*, 40″ x 64″, copyright 1985 by Flavin Glover. Photograph by Glenn R. Glover.

FOUR PATCH: CONTEMPORARY

Flavin Glover has turned to nature and adjusted the basic Four Patch pattern to conform to the outline of her *Fourth Forest*. As in her other quilts (see page 25), the careful blending of fabrics has given this wall hanging a three-dimensional effect. Three large triangular areas of dark green printed cottons represent trees at the bottom of the quilt. As the eye moves toward the top of the piece, the "trees" become smaller, move closer together, and are less defined, giving a sense of depth to the picture. In this quilt, each Four Patch block has been pieced separately and is set on the diagonal. The absence of the alternating "in-between" block, as seen in the traditional version on page 26, makes the hanging appear to have been based on a One Patch pattern.

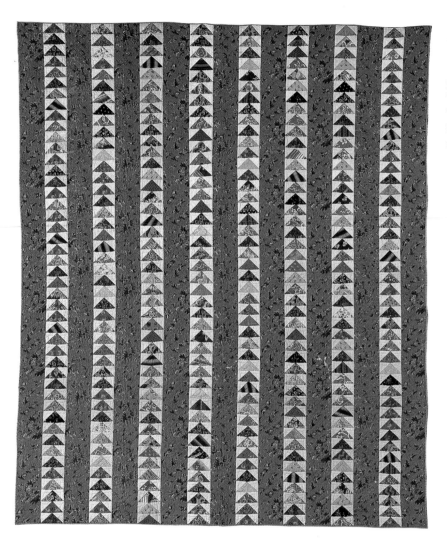

27. Flying Geese, 97″ x 81″, c. 1840, from the Williams family of New Jersey. Quilt courtesy Tracy Jamar, Jamar Textile Restoration Studio, New York City. Photography copyright 1986 by Schecter Lee.

FLYING GEESE: TRADITIONAL

Flying Geese has always been a very popular pattern used both for a full quilt or for just a border. Because of its flexibility in width and in length, it adapts easily to many quilts, traditional and contemporary alike. The antique quilt shown here is a perfect example of the Flying Geese pattern used throughout a quilt in strips that alternate with printed fabric. The use of a white background for the patchwork provides a sharp contrast to the brown print in the sashing. Large triangles in a wide assortment of prints make this elegant scrap-bag quilt a fine collection of fabrics, dating around 1840–1850.

Rachel Van Riper Williams and husband John Williams of New Jersey were the original owners of the quilt, and it is believed that Rachel may have been the quiltmaker.

Rachel Van Riper Williams owned considerable land in New Jersey from the original land grant given her ancestors in 1664. On November 17, 1800, Rachel married John Williams in Second River, New Jersey, a town later renamed Belleville. John Williams was an importer, which may explain the variety and excellent choice of fabrics used in the quilt. John was also a banker and owner of the riverboat that ran on the Passaic River to Newark, New Jersey.

The quilt has never been washed, for it had been little used. There are a few fragile areas in the brown printed fabric, and the quilt is bound with handwoven tape, which was frequently done on quilts of this period.

28. *Bird Wars: The Origin of Super Goose*, 57″ x 41″, copyright 1986 by Nancy Dice, Bellevue, Washington.

FLYING GEESE: CONTEMPORARY

Bird Wars: The Origin of Super Goose, designed and made by Nancy Dice of Bellevue, Washington, is based on the amusingly imaginative transformation of a simple flight of Flying Geese into a flock of superhero geese, after a battle with birds of another feather. Containing every comic-book cliché the artist could think of, the result is a sprightly amalgam of traditional and contemporary gone slightly haywire.

NANCY DICE: "I wanted to do a 'comic-book' quilt and it had to have at least a semblance of a story line. One of the most common clichés of comic art is the origin of a superhero.

"Since I really like geese, I decided to make a goose my hero and have him be transformed from a simple innocuous flying goose, just flying along, minding his own business, into Super Goose, complete with badge on his chest. The quilt also uses my original block of a sort of bird (from my quilt *When the Pie Was Opened*) as the evil attacker who is defeated by Super Goose. There are lightning bolts, explosions, laser beams (metallic silver thread couched on to the surface), embroidered eyeballs, and buttons as the points under exclamation and question marks."

Bird Wars: The Origin of Super Goose was selected to be displayed as part of "Surface Design Northwest: A Juried Regional Competition" in Seattle, Washington, and was entered in the annual Pacific Northwest Arts and Crafts Fair Juried Exhibit in 1986, where it received the prize for the Crafts/Textiles division. Following the exhibition, it was hung in the Bellevue Art Museum along with other prizewinners.

29. Clam Shell, 74″ x 74″, made in 1864 by Mrs. Mary Boyer of McLeod County, Minnesota. Joyce Aufderheide Collection. Photograph by E. Rousseau.

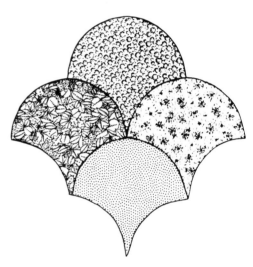

CLAM SHELL: TRADITIONAL

Use of the Clam Shell pattern in this country originated in the Cape Cod, Massachusetts, area, but many older quilts containing this shape (either quilted or pieced) can be found in or traced back to England and Europe. In her book *Old Patchwork Quilts and the Women Who Made Them*, Ruth Finley states that because of the difficulty of piecing the many curves of this pattern, it has been used very little since the early 1800s.

This unusual version of the Clam Shell pattern was made in 1864 by Mrs. Mary Boyer in McLeod County, Minnesota. The top, quilted in the 1930s, has dark and light stripes created with the Clam Shell units.

An interesting assortment of calicoes, plaids, ginghams, and stripes are used in this quilt and date it to the turn of the century. Many brown fabrics have been used in the quilt and are in excellent condition, a sure sign that this quilt has been well preserved. Brown fabrics from antique quilts of this age are often frayed and disintegrated due to the type of dye that was used to obtain the color. The edges of the quilt have been turned to the inside and blind-stitched, sparing the quiltmaker the difficulty of manipulating a binding around the many curves and points found at the edges.

CLAM SHELL: CONTEMPORARY

Pat Cox's *Four Seasons Clam Shell Appliqué*, a wonderful wall hanging, is an excellent example of how today's quilters are "freshening up" old patterns. Pat has made a series of appliquéd pictures based on the Clam Shell pattern, and her *Four Seasons* quilt is her most ambitious use of the pattern.

PAT COX: "The Clam Shell pattern has always intrigued me; as I was working on a quilt, it suddenly came to me how I could use it in an entirely different application.

By shading the appliqué pieces just right, I was able to use the pattern for a section of water in a drawing."

The unusual setting of the four circular scenes in Pat's quilt is balanced and enhanced by her clever use of appliquéd motifs, including leaves, flowers, and snowflakes.

Pat is the owner of One of a Kind Quilting Designs, a business she has formed to promote her wonderful patterns, including those used to make her Clam Shell designs.

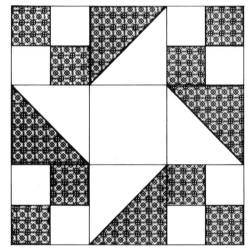

31. Snail's Trail, 72″ x 68″, c. 1870. Quilt courtesy Wild Goose Chase Quilt Gallery, Evanston, Illinois. Photograph by Schecter Lee.

MONKEY WRENCH OR SNAIL'S TRAIL: TRADITIONAL

Gail Struve, owner of the Wild Goose Chase Quilt Gallery in Evanston, Illinois, picked up this mustard-yellow and white Snail's Trail quilt to add to her impressive stock of antique quilts. Supposedly made by a quilter living in Huntington, Indiana, this quilt dates to the 1870s. Also called Indiana Puzzle, this quilt is a variation of the traditional Monkey Wrench pattern shown above, Fewer pieces per block make this much easier and faster to piece.

The Monkey Wrench pattern, and its derivatives, is one that has been around for some time, but it is not frequently used. Research in several quilting publications turned up just two examples of the simple version of this design. *First, Nine and Always* by Millie Leathers has a red and white Indiana Puzzle on page 42, with patterned blocks alternating with white squares on the diagonal. David Pottinger's book *Quilts from the Indiana Amish* shows an Indiana Puzzle quilt on page 58 that appears to be the twin to a quilt owned by Akron, Ohio, collector Darwin Bearly.

The quilt shown here is made of a 100 percent cotton print in mustard-yellow combined with unbleached muslin. A single white border has been finished with a wide binding of the printed fabric. A single square in each of the four corners of the quilt, followed by a round-corner binding, is a rather unusual corner treatment.

The basic pattern for Monkey Wrench is given on page 87.

32. *Monkey Wrench I*, 96″ x 96″, copyright 1978 by Pamela Gustavson Johnson, Kansas City, Missouri. Photograph by E. G. Schempf.

MONKEY WRENCH OR SNAIL'S TRAIL: CONTEMPORARY

Pamela Gustavson Johnson of Kansas City, Missouri, has been quilting for some time now, but it is during the last five years that her work has caught the eyes of publishers and editors nationwide. Pamela's *Monkey Wrench* shown here is just one of her many interesting and unusual creations. By adjusting the pattern so that it becomes smaller as it flows toward the center of the quilt, she has created a three-dimensional effect.

PAMELA GUSTAVSON JOHNSON: "Quilts have often been described as important cultural documents that reflect the women who made them and the times in which they were made. This is quite a statement and one that is a considerable challenge to live up to. Simply repeating traditional patterns does not address this vital purpose.

"I enjoy making use of 'traditional' patterns as a starting point, to make reference to the past, but feel that these old forms must be reinterpreted within one's own frame of reference."

Four printed fabrics have been combined to repeat the spinning Monkey Wrench shape in varying degrees of light and dark, and each shape has been echo-quilted to further emphasize these changes. Four borders matching the colors in the quilt set off the design in a simple but effective manner.

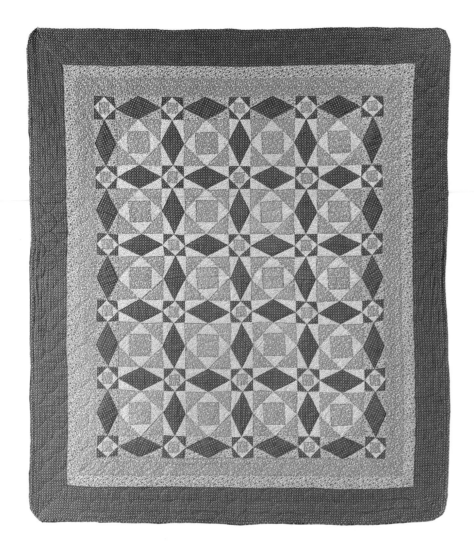

33. Storm at Sea, 95″ x 85″. The top for this quilt was made in 1983 by Betty Boyink. It was then quilted by the United Methodist Church of the Dunes quilting group. Quilt courtesy Reini Moser, Nunica, Michigan. Photograph by Schecter Lee.

STORM AT SEA: TRADITIONAL

The Storm at Sea pattern has gained its popularity during the last fifty years. Published in the *Ladies Art Company*, number 135, Storm at Sea was seldom seen in quilts before that time. Because of its nautical theme, this pattern is usually made in shades of blue, and, if carefully selected, the fabrics will simulate a sense of motion between the colors in the blocks. It is probably because of this motion that contemporary quiltmakers have found the Storm at Sea pattern so exciting.

Although the quilt shown here is not old, it is a very traditional example of the pattern. The top, made of 18-inch-square blocks and three surrounding borders in shades of blue and tan, was pieced by Betty Boyink of Grand Haven, Michigan, in 1982. It was then quilted by the United Methodist Church of the Dunes quilting group, also of Grand Haven, and purchased at the church's Fall Bazaar by Reini Moser of Nunica, Michigan.

A pattern for a Storm at Sea block can be found on page 84.

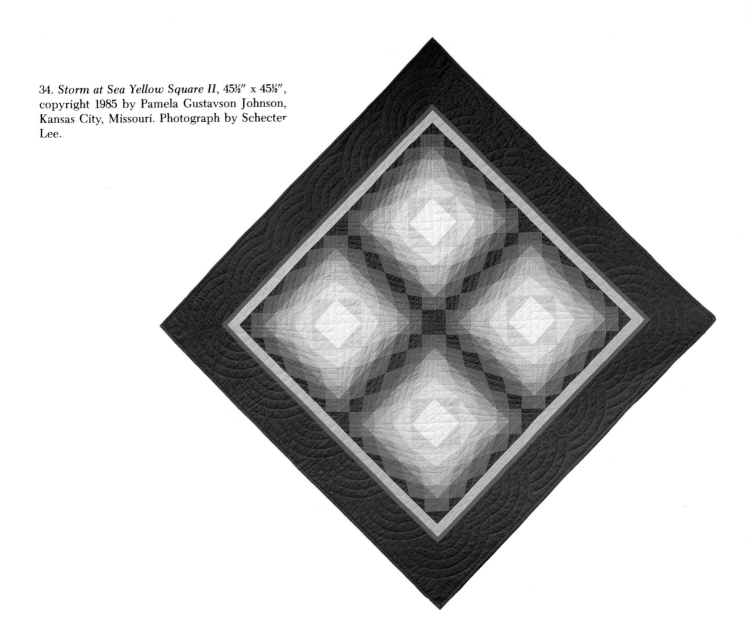

STORM AT SEA: CONTEMPORARY

Another quilt by Pamela Gustavson Johnson is this bright optical illusion, *Storm at Sea Yellow Square II*, machine-pieced and hand-quilted in 1985. Pamela has done such a wonderful job drafting and choosing the fabrics for this "distorted" Storm at Sea that it almost hurts your eyes to stare at it for very long (an effect she, no doubt, was trying to achieve!).

Made of 100 percent cotton fabrics, *Storm at Sea Yellow Square II* is set "on point" rather than in the traditional straight setting. Simple borders of solid fabrics repeat the colors used in the pattern, and the traditional fan quilting motif has been applied to the outermost border.

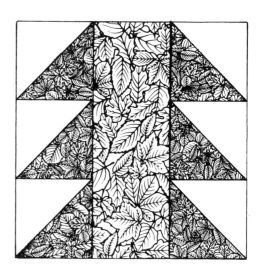

35. Tree Everlasting, 45″ x 43″, c. 1800. Collection of John R. Sauls, Tyler, Texas. Photograph courtesy J. R. Sauls.

TREE EVERLASTING: TRADITIONAL

This primitive crib quilt was made around 1850 of bright red and vegetable-dyed green solid fabrics. John Sauls, an antiques dealer from Tyler, Texas, found the quilt in Cumberland County, Pennsylvania, and added it to his large collection of antique quilts.

The Tree Everlasting pattern is very simple to assemble, for it is formed by sewing a simple sawtooth row of squares to either side of a wider, solid piece of fabric. The alternating rows of dark and light fabrics produce the sharp contrast that makes this pattern so dramatic.

In this piece the quilting consists of diagonal rows of stitching across the patterns and chevron quilting along the borders. The imbalance of the pattern on the left side of the quilt makes it an interesting addition to any collection.

36. *Spring Storm*, 48½″ x 46″, made in 1984 by Margery Cosgrove. Photograph by Schecter Lee.

TREE EVERLASTING: CONTEMPORARY

Margery Cosgrove, of Cincinnati, Ohio, has hidden her "touch of tradition" in this contemporary quilt called *Spring Storm*. Serving as trees in this fabric painting, the Tree Everlasting pattern provides a beautiful backdrop for the horses who gallop across the center of the quilt.

Margery's fascinating handling of shapes and color takes us right into the country, where the sun and an approaching storm vie for our interest. Freely stitched quilting lines add to the feeling of freedom and motion in the piece. Subtle shades in the plaid border are a relaxing finish to this interesting quilt.

Margery has been an active seamstress since the age of ten, attempting her first quilt in the mid-1970s. Her education and career have focused primarily on art and design; she majored in fabric design at The Art Institute of Chicago and has done freelance design for both Intermedia Advertising and Procter & Gamble. She has been published in *Ecclesiastical Crafts* by Bucky King, the *Goodfellow Catalog of Wonderful Things*, *Woman's Day* magazine, *Fiberarts*, and *Quilter's Newsletter Magazine*.

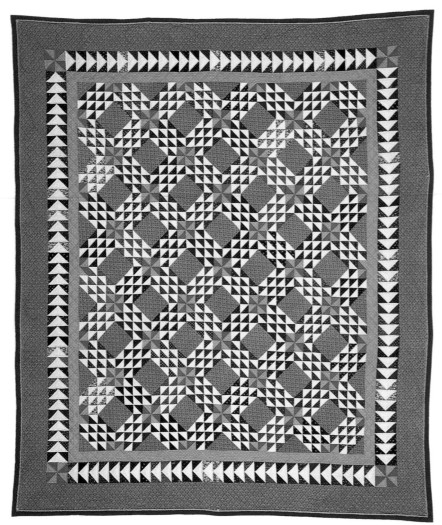

37. Ocean Waves, 97″ x 80″, made in 1985 by the author. Photograph by E. Rousseau.

OCEAN WAVES: TRADITIONAL

Ocean Waves is a pattern that has been popular for many generations. Inspired by an antique quilt on the cover of the April 1983 issue of *Country Living*, I decided to make my own version of the pattern. Dark green and blue prints blend together to surround a medium-brown printed fabric, with additions of rust and gold set to form a Pinwheel design throughout the quilt. A border of Flying Geese echoes the prints and triangular shapes in the center of the quilt creating a strong "country" appearance, which was my basic idea for the project. Cross-hatching, quilted every half-inch, fills each of the large squares, with outline quilting around each of the 2,348 triangles. A curved design follows the edges of the quilt in quarter-inch echo-quilting, giving the appearance of trapunto, although the quilting has not been stuffed.

38. *Washed Out to See*, 40″ x 40″, made in 1986 by the author. Photograph by Charles Scroggins.

OCEAN WAVES: CONTEMPORARY

Designed to be a play on words, *Washed Out to See* was made following a successful introduction to the process of home-dyeing fabric. This wall quilt is based on the traditional Ocean Waves pattern, although several areas of the quilt have been altered to obtain the desired effect. An example of deviating from the traditional block pattern (shown on page 38) can be found in the center of the quilt, where several pieced triangles have replaced the usual square set on point that is formed by joining several blocks together.

The gradation of dark blue to light blue has been used to simulate the changing colors of the ocean from out in deep water to where the waves splash on the shore. The addition of small amounts of silver lamé and clumps of glittering beads represents the sun's glinting on the water. The use of machine-quilting with silver metallic thread in a freeform design adds additional sparkles to the "water."

39. Kansas Dugout, 72″ x 58″, c. 1880. Quilt courtesy Adelaide F. Wasserman, Homewood, Illinois. Photograph by N. Dean Mosey, Jr.

KANSAS DUGOUT: TRADITIONAL

Although it is hard to spot at first glance, the quilt shown here is a variation of the Kansas Dugout pattern shown in the diagram above. Strips of deep maroon velvet have been used in each block, giving the effect of lattice striping. Four triangles have been pieced with heavy cloth of numerous designs; they replace the traditional plain square in the center. Shimmery beige fabric quilted with two shades of heavy pearl cotton thread provides decoration in the solid blocks.

This Kansas Dugout, made in a style similar to the elaborate Crazy quilts popular in the late 1800s, was purchased in Indiana and is a favorite quilt in the collection of Adelaide Wasserman of Homewood, Illinois.

ADELAIDE WASSERMAN: "I find two things particularly interesting about this quilt: the care its creator took in working out the balance of color and fabric, and the placement of the different diamonds. What first caught my eye when I saw its folded end on the shelf at the store still delights me every time I look at it—the contrast of the deep colored bands and the brilliant diamond shapes between them make the whole thing shine like a collection of jewels. It's a real beauty and its maker must have had a true artist's feeling for color. She must have been quite a person."

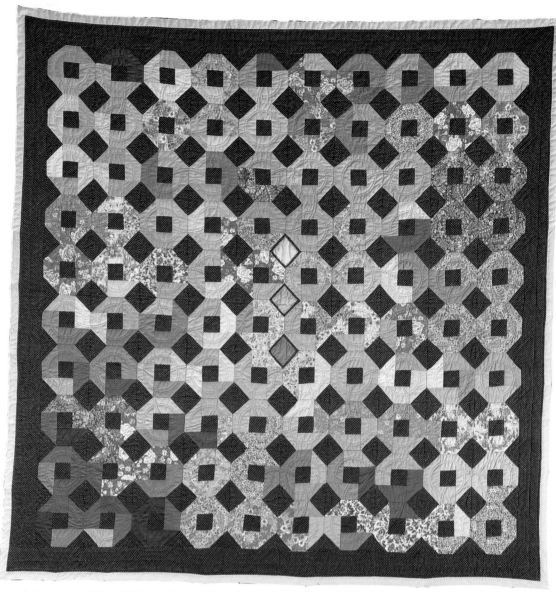

40. *Passages*, 68½″ x 67½″, made in 1979 by Virginia Randles, Athens, Ohio. Photograph by Schecter Lee.

KANSAS DUGOUT: CONTEMPORARY

Virginia Randles of Athens, Ohio, has devoted her career to designing and making contemporary quilts. One of her pieces, made in 1979, is based on a variation of the Kansas Dugout pattern. In her *Passages*, Virginia has used a pieced background of dark blue and neutral dotted fabric with a variety of print and solid-color fabrics in a free arrangement of colors. The dark fabrics used in *Passages* recede into the quilt, making the color patches seem to "pop out" toward the viewer. Three squares in the center have been framed with black strips, thus ensuring their receiving special attention.

While many quiltmakers prefer working with 100 percent cotton fabrics because of their ease in quiltability, Virginia leans toward a cotton-blend broadcloth or similar fabrics for their sheen and resiliency in quilting. For contrast, she claims that she has "used 100 percent cottons for their dullness as well as other qualities."

As a quilter, Virginia has had her work published in just about every quilt magazine, as well as in several books, including *The New American Quilt*, *Ohio Quilts: A Living Tradition*, and *A Garden of Quilts*. She was featured in the "Quilting I" and "Quilting II" television series from Bowling Green, Ohio, and some of her quilts are owned by both private and corporate collections.

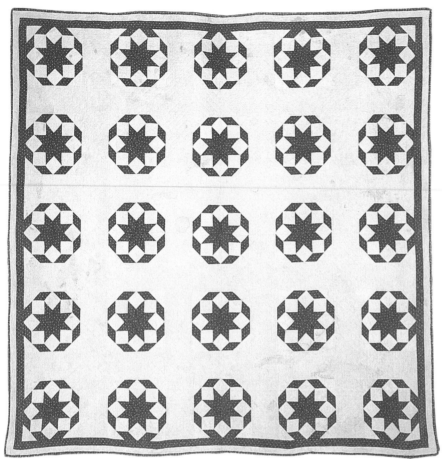

41. Rolling Star, 77″ x 75½″, c. 1870. Quilt courtesy Spencer Museum of Art, The University of Kansas; Gift of Clara Gillham. Photograph by Jon Blumb.

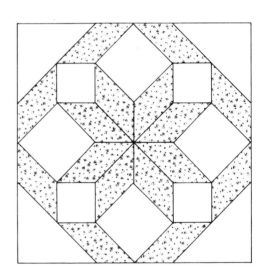

ROLLING STAR: TRADITIONAL

This beautiful blue and white Rolling Star quilt is part of the collection of the Spencer Museum of Art at the University of Kansas. Although it was given to the museum as a gift by Clara Gillham in 1927, little information is available on the date or maker of the quilt. It is possible that the quilt was made by Clara's mother around 1870.

Precise piecing of the blue print fabric and muslin, combined with simple crosshatched quilting lines, make this a very handsome piece. A double border in the same fabrics contributes to the bold graphic statement made by the quilt.

42. *Rolling Star Breakdown*, 40″ x 43½″. Copyright 1986 by Nancy Smeltzer.

ROLLING STAR: CONTEMPORARY

Rolling Star Breakdown is one of a series of quilts Nancy Smeltzer of Columbia, Maryland, is doing in collaboration with Florida quiltmaker Deanna Powell. In preparation for a future exhibition, Nancy and Deanna have been working on several small projects in which they choose a traditional pattern, agree on colors, and then execute their own interpretation of the pattern. *Rolling Star Breakdown* is the first quilt to come off Nancy's frame in preparation for the exhibition.

Working jointly with another quiltmaker can be a real challenge, as Nancy has quickly learned.

NANCY SMELTZER: "Without seeing Deanna's fabric or placement of the patterns, I made my fabric color choices based on the swatches she sent me. Try as hard as I can sometimes to tone down my color choices, I find I'm the happiest when my colors jump out at the viewer. My guess is that we may have some difficulty in hanging the two quilts [together] in a future show, as Powell tends to work with a more subdued palette than I do.

"When I work, I have no preplanned idea of how the finished piece will look. I made the three traditional blocks, and then pinned them into place on the lavender background. I wanted it to look as if some of the blocks had unraveled, hence the 'Breakdown' part of the name."

In 1977, Nancy received her MFA in Art Teacher Education at Maryland Institute College of Art. In talking about her educational accomplishments, Nancy was quick to share the fact that she had to count the number of hours that she spent on a quilt as a final part of her MFA, because the head of the department didn't think that fiber arts took enough time to justify a degree. She was able to convince him that 650 hours on one piece was certainly enough time to devote to any art form. In expressing her devotion to the craft, Nancy stated that "While I have tried most of the artistic media in art school, nothing gives me quite the same thrill as running my hands over fabric."

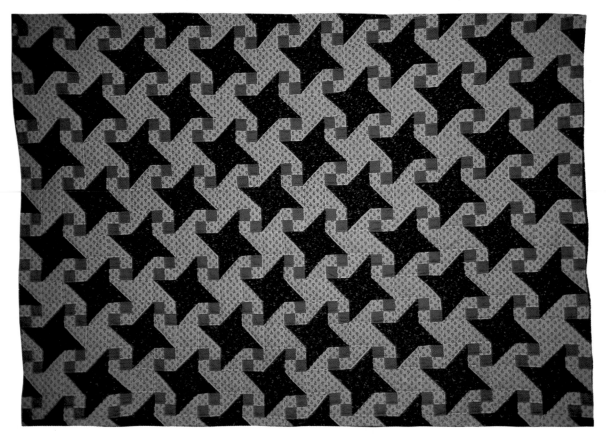

43. Milky Way, 96″ x 84″, made in 1981 by Marion Wheelock, Irving, Texas. Photograph by Award Photography, Irving, Texas.

MILKY WAY: TRADITIONAL

The Milky Way pattern is very similar to Indiana Puzzle and Monkey Wrench, and it is sometimes called Chinese Corn. The quilt shown here was made by Marion Wheelock of Irving, Texas, in 1981. Marion used pattern #3540, found in *Aunt Martha's Quilt Lovers' Delight,* to make her templates for piecing the quilt.

Marion chose to use autumn-colored fabrics in her Milky Way, selecting a white print with orange and brown flowers to complement the 100 percent cotton brown print and solid orange fabrics. Outline quilting has been used as a complement to this repetitive design, and a dark brown binding doubles as a border.

As a quiltmaker, Marion has had over ten years of experience. Although she won a blue ribbon for a Sampler Quilt she made, this is the first time that one of her quilts has been published. She is a member of the Dallas Quilter's Guild and the mother of five children.

44. *Meanwhile, in Another Part of the Galaxy...* 56″ x 40″, copyright 1986 by Nancy Dice.

MILKY WAY: CONTEMPORARY

Nancy Dice has turned the easily pieced Milky Way pattern into a quilt that all "outer space" enthusiasts should find amusing. Her quilt, titled *Meanwhile, in Another Part of the Galaxy . . .*, uses Milky Way as a background. The basic Milky Way blocks have been blown up to an eight-inch size and put together with strip-piecing techniques. Tinker-toy space stations and silver lamé wind-up men with silver-cording air tubes are appliquéd over the top.

Nancy has exhibited in many northwestern galleries, including the American Gallery of Quilt and Textile Art in Gig Harbor, Washington. Her quilts, reflecting a style all her own, have been included in *Diamond Patchwork* by Jeffrey Gutcheon, and in *Quilter's Newsletter Magazine*. Nancy has also done the quilting on some of the pieces Marsha McCloskey has included in her books *Wall Quilts* and *Small Quilts*.

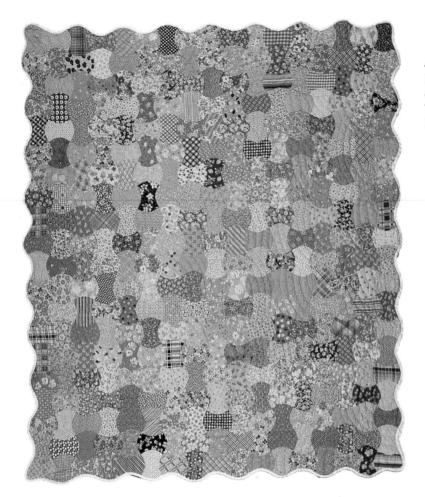

45. Ax Head or Spools, 87½″ x 73½″. Made by Marian Dixon Harston, 1930–1935. Quilt courtesy Melinda Hamm Giacomarro, Hurst, Texas. Photograph by Gilstrap Photography, Hurst, Texas.

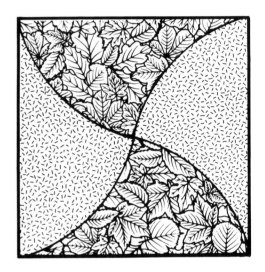

AX HEAD: TRADITIONAL

The quilt shown here is known by many different names: Ax Head, Badge of Friendship, Jigsaw, Mother's Oddity, Spools, Friendship Quilt, Charm Quilt, and many more. Made of continuously curving patches as the diagram above shows, it is not an easy quilt for a beginner to sew. The easiest method of piecing this pattern is to sew the "spool" shapes into long strips, and then sew one row to another. Because of the number of edges that are cut on the bias, careful handling of the pieces is a must!

Ax Head, as this quilt is called by its owner Melinda Giacomarro of Hurst, Texas, was made between 1930 and 1935 by Melinda's grandmother. Marian Dixon Harston of Fort Worth, Texas, presented this quilt and two other scrap quilts to her granddaughter in 1970. In mint condition, the quilt boasts a scalloped border that follows the edges of the Ax Head pieces.

46. *Captured Rainbow*, 42″ x 42″, made in 1980 by Margery Cosgrove. Photograph by Schecter Lee.

AX HEAD: CONTEMPORARY

At first glance it is hard to determine the pattern that *Captured Rainbow* is based on. In fact, its creator, Margery Cosgrove, was not aware of the pattern name when she began the quilt in 1980 in a workshop taught by Michael James. It was not until the fall of 1986 that we discovered (and it's so easy to see now!) that this quilt is based on the Ax Head or Spools pattern. Although Margery divided and pieced the quilt into square blocks, when all the blocks were placed side by side, the spool shapes emerged.

Another quilt by Margery Cosgrove may be found on page 13.

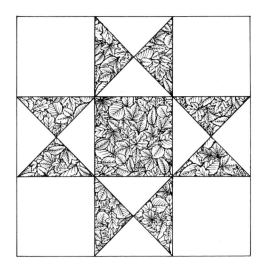

47. Ohio Star, 80″ x 74″, c. 1890. Quilt courtesy Tracy Jamar, Jamar Textile Restoration Studio, New York City. Photograph by E. Rousseau.

OHIO STAR: TRADITIONAL

The Ohio Star pattern is a very popular design that can be traced back to the late 1700s. This scrap quilt, owned by Tracy Jamar of Jamar Textile Restoration Studio in New York City, dates to the 1890s and is believed to have been made in Ohio.

An excellent selection of fabrics from the late 1800s forms the stars in each block. Pink printed fabric has been used in the solid blocks and in the border to give a sense of uniformity to the quilt. The excellent condition of the quilt indicates that it was used very seldom, if at all. Pencil lines used to mark the quilting motifs are still visible, and it has never been washed. The quilt has been all hand-pieced and hand-quilted except for along the borders and bindings, which have been machine-sewn. Accurate piecing helps give the quilt a very crisp, fresh look.

The Ohio Star pattern is often found in old Amish quilts. Many beautiful examples of Amish Ohio Star quilts can be found in David Pottinger's book *Quilts from the Indiana Amish*.

48. *The Light*, 68″ x 68″, copyright 1984 by Lil Golston. Photograph courtesy the artist.

OHIO STAR: CONTEMPORARY

Two pattern names come to mind when inspecting this quilt, called *The Light*, by Lil Golston. The first is Ohio Star, a design most quiltmakers are familiar with. The other is Joseph's Coat. Joseph's Coat is more difficult to spot than Ohio Star, because the Ohio Star design is more familiar to us and the dark colors that form the stars draw our eye to that portion of the quilt.

Most of the "modernizing" of traditional quilts that Lil has done has been inspired by Judy Martin's *Patchworkbook*. As Lil says, "I find that using traditional patterns helps keep my contemporary work 'down to earth.' My

goal is to make quilts that are a pleasure to live with, and I find this blend of old and new quilt pleasing."

All of the fabrics used to create *The Light* are 100 percent cotton prints in varying shades of blue, bright yellow, and gold, which, in combination with circular quilting motifs, draw the eye toward the center of the quilt.

The Light has been exhibited in Colombia, South America, in an exhibition curated by Janet Elwin, and was hung in the 1986 Paducah, Kentucky, show as well as in the National Patchwork Championships in England.

49. One Patch, 80″ x 66½″, c. 1930. Collection of N. Dean and Caron L. Mosey. Photograph by Schecter Lee.

ONE PATCH: TRADITIONAL

This pale pink quilt in the One Patch pattern dates back to the 1930s and is notable for the wide assortment of attractive and eye-catching printed fabrics from that period that it contains.

The quilt has a very pleasing balanced design featuring a framed center square placed on point and two wide pastel borders enlivened by the two One Patch borders. The quilt has been hand-pieced and hand-quilted with a heavy cotton batting. Although the quilting stitches are not tiny, they are very even and form a simple cable

design in the border and the long pink strips of the quilt.

Many One Patch designs are similar to the Postage Stamp pattern shown earlier in this book, but the size of the individual squares is usually 1½ inches square or larger. Often made in an overall design, the One Patch is a good pattern to use when making a scrap or charm quilt. Because of the simplicity in construction, the One Patch has been used for several hundred years as a utility quilt, and many a youngster has learned to piece using this pattern.

50. *Chubby Checkers*, 21½″ x 21½″, copyright 1986 by Ami Simms, Flint, Michigan. Photograph by Charles Scroggins.

ONE PATCH: CONTEMPORARY

Tiny but amusing and dynamic, *Chubby Checkers* by Ami Simms is a takeoff on the traditional One Patch pattern. The design for *Chubby Checkers* was drafted by Ami and her mother, Beebe Moss, and later hand-appliquéd and quilted by Ami.

AMI SIMMS: "This particular piece was an experiment to see if one could appliqué (using an invisible ladder stitch) a pieced design. Before designing this quilt, I began playing around with shapes and forms to have

some fun. *Chubby Checkers* was the result of one of my 'playtimes.'"

Ami works almost exclusively with 100 percent cotton solid fabrics and is noted for her minute quilting stitches. She has had several articles and quilts published since her quilting career began more than eleven years ago, and has recently written and published three books: *Invisible Appliqué*, *Little Ditties*, and *How to Improve Your Quilting Stitch*.

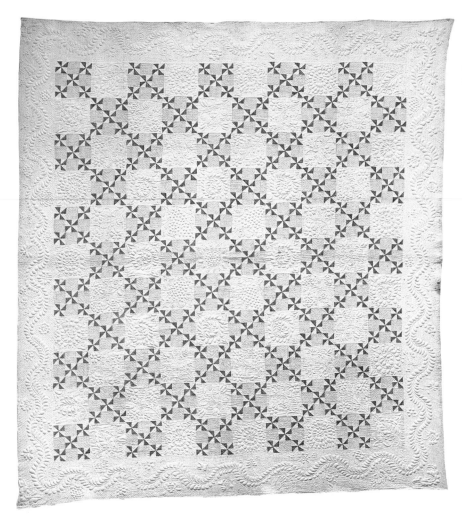

51. Pinwheel, 94″ x 85″, c. 1812. Collection of Smithsonian Institution, Washington, D.C.

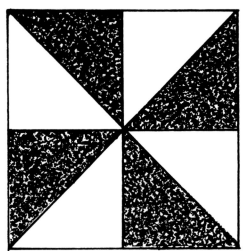

PINWHEEL: TRADITIONAL

A single triangle template is all that is necessary to make a quilt in the Pinwheel pattern. Made as a two-tone quilt or as a charming scrap quilt, the Pinwheel has been around for over 150 years.

The beautiful Pinwheel shown here is from the collection of the Smithsonian Institution, Washington, D.C. Blue and white Pinwheel blocks have been pieced with pale pink squares, forming Nine Patch blocks. The quilt, said to have been made by the women of a Maryland family while their men were away during the War of 1812, is beautifully decorated with several different quilting motifs, including feather wreaths and grapes, all of which have been rendered in stuffed work (also called trapunto). A serpentine feather motif embellishes the borders of the quilt, and small motifs have been fitted into the "hills and valleys" of the serpentine stuffed work. It is an elegant creation and considering the age of the piece, it is in marvelous condition.

Patterns for Pinwheel blocks in two sizes can be found on page 83.

52. *Sparklers*, 45″ x 45″, copyright 1983 by Carla Rodio. Photograph by Schecter Lee.

PINWHEEL: CONTEMPORARY

Sparklers, designed and made by Carla Rodio of Utica, New York, is based on the ever-popular Pinwheel pattern. This 1983 machine-pieced quilt was part of an early quest for color and design in quiltmaking. Some patches from an earlier quilt, *Splendor*, were used in this diagonally set design.

The Pinwheel design has also been set into the border of *Sparklers*, as if the pinwheels were spinning off the quilt. Warm rust and green in 100 percent cotton have been effectively contrasted with the lighter sashing strips and piecing in the center of the quilt. The process of quilting

is not as important to Carla as the design element, so the quilting was handled by Carol Sambora. When asked why she does not do her own quilting, she said, "It takes too long. I'm not that great as a hand stitcher. My interest is in the total visual impact, not details of technique."

Owner and manager of Quilters' Comfort in Utica, New York, Carla has been exhibiting her work since 1980. In 1980 she received a certificate of Special Studies in Textile Arts from the Fiberworks Center for Textile Arts, and has studied with Nancy Crow, Michael James, and Maria McCormick Snyder.

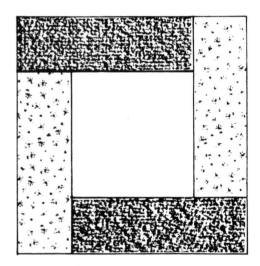

53. Bright Hopes, 18″ x 15½″, made in 1986 by the author. Photograph by N. Dean Mosey, Jr.

BRIGHT HOPES: TRADITIONAL

Because of the simplicity of the design, the Bright Hopes pattern adapts well to a small format, as is seen in the quilt shown here. Tiny three-inch-square blocks sewn together by hand are a perfect size to cover a child's doll, or to serve as a small accent on a country kitchen wall.

The fabrics chosen for this scrap quilt are a random sampling of antique fabrics mixed with fresh-off-the-bolt 1980s prints. To achieve a uniform appearance, the newer fabrics have been dyed with tea to tone down any harshness caused by bright colors or stark white backgrounds in the prints. A quarter-inch border of muslin, followed by an inch of antique 100 percent cotton print serves as a good ending to this little girl's delight.

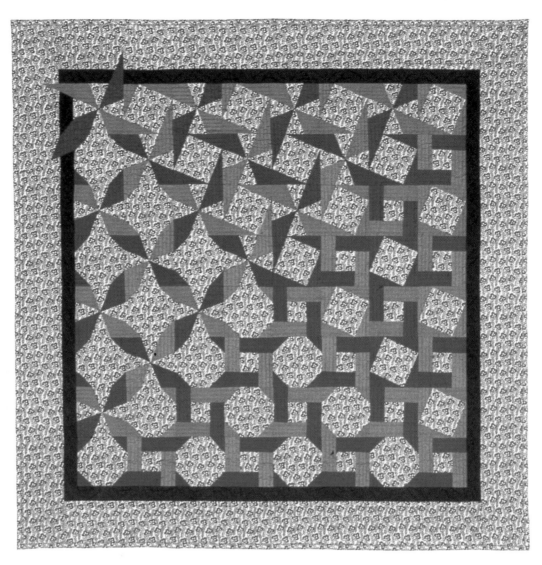

54. *Social Interaction*, 40″ x 40″, copyright 1982 by Pamela Gustavson Johnson, Kansas City, Missouri. Photograph by E. G. Schempf.

BRIGHT HOPES: CONTEMPORARY

Bright Hopes, or Round the Twist, has been combined with two other blocks based on a square grid to form Pamela Gustavson Johnson's quilt *Social Interaction*. Design elements in *Social Interaction* are similar to those used by the same artist in *Reflections on Arnheim* (see page 2), where the basic design unit is gradually altered.

Three well-chosen fabrics form the design in this wall hanging, and are set off with the addition of a black border. Not all of the pattern is contained within the border, however; in the upper left corner several pieces of the pattern seem to be trying to "escape" from the confines of the border. It is a fascinating piece.

Social Interaction was on display in Japan as a part of the "Contemporary American Quilts in Japan" invitational exhibition, and it is featured in the catalogue of that show.

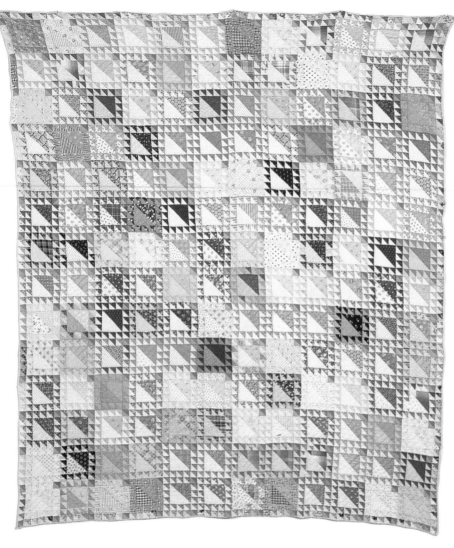

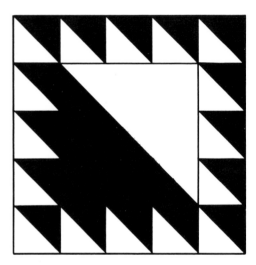

55. Lady of the Lake, 77″ x 68″, c. 1910. Collection of N. Dean and Caron L. Mosey. Photograph by E. Rousseau.

LADY OF THE LAKE: TRADITIONAL

Thousands of triangles measuring less than one inch on a side were sewn together by a quiltmaker in the early 1900s to make this scrap-bag quilt. Called Lady of the Lake, this pattern is one that has been in existence since the early 1800s. Because of the small pieces it was a very useful pattern, for one could effectively use all the tiny snippets of fabric that were too small to include in patterns where large patches were required.

The quilter who made this utility quilt skillfully added a touch of gold and rust at the corners of each block, thus providing a sense of unity to the jumble of fabrics she had to work with. A heavily woven fabric serves as a lining, and though the batting is very thin, evidence of cotton seeds shows through the worn spots. Handwoven tape has been used as a binding, and quilting has been done in straight lines.

56. *Lady of the Lake*, 35″ x 35″, copyright 1986 by Caron L. Mosey. Photograph by N. Dean Mosey, Jr.

LADY OF THE LAKE: CONTEMPORARY

Meant to be a play on words, a close look at this pictorial quilt reveals a grid based on the traditional Lady of the Lake design. By the careful changing of color and the gradation of blue from dark to light, the images of a lake and shoreline have been created. The tall, slender woman standing at the edge of the lake represents fond memories of my summers as a teenager, spent gazing out at the water in northern Michigan. It also represents my desire to be svelte, chic, and glamorous (dream on!). The quilting in *Lady of the Lake* follows the horizontal lines of the horizon, but gracefully dips and swirls to show a slight breeze.

Lady of the Lake was exhibited for the first time in February 1987 at the Citizens Bank Lobby Gallery in Flint, Michigan, during a one-woman exhibition titled "New Quilts by Caron Mosey."

57. Crazy Quilt, 55″ x 55″, c. 1895, maker unknown. Collection of N. Dean and Caron L. Mosey. Photograph by E. Rousseau.

CRAZY QUILT: TRADITIONAL

There are as many different ways to assemble a Crazy Quilt as there are quilters to make them. The diagram above has been included to give you an example of the random placement of fabrics in a typical Crazy Quilt. A standard Crazy Quilt is made in square segments. Each square is arranged, embroidered, and finally sewn to the connecting squares. It is the wide assortment of elegant fabrics and intricate embroidery that make a Crazy Quilt so appealing. Velvet, silk, ribbon, taffeta, and other fabrics shimmer beautifully when they are embellished with delicate embroidered motifs.

The Crazy Quilt shown here boasts a potpourri of embroidered designs. Owls, horseshoes, butterflies, and many different flowers have been tastefully stitched to the quilt's surface. Two separate monograms of the letter R and a large monogram with the letters F A S are included; perhaps a hint that this quilt was made by more than one needleworker. Campaign ribbons with photographs of Cleveland and Thurman, Benjamin Harrison and Levi Morton, as well as a ribbon from the Thirty-fifth Annual Session of the Grand Lodge of I.O. of G.T. of Michigan (October 16, 17, 18, 1888) are also included.

For a thorough discussion of this fascinating quilt genre, consult *Crazy Quilts* by Penny McMorris.

58. *Crazy Quilt #4*, 93″ x 60″, made in 1986 by Elizabeth Miller, Chauncey, Ohio. Photograph copyright by John Sattler.

CRAZY QUILT: CONTEMPORARY

Elizabeth Miller of Chauncey, Ohio, has paid tribute to antique Crazy Quilts with her unusual version shown here. Although the quilt retains the "crazy" look, the embellishments used to spice up the fabrics are somewhat out of the ordinary. Stuffed appliqué, flowers, buttons, beads, sequins, parts of earrings, and small keys are used in addition to embroidery. Areas of the quilt have been painted to achieve just the right look, and lattice strips connect the twelve blocks together. It is a charming, colorful, and fascinating composition.

59. House, 82″ x 72″, 1900-1910. Photograph courtesy America Hurrah Antiques, New York City.

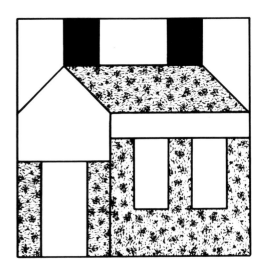

HOUSE: TRADITIONAL

Many variations of the House pattern have been made through the years, each seeming to be as individual as the quiltmaker who created it. Using the idea of incorporating a building in each block, quilts have been made that show barns, churches, schools—indeed, all sorts of structures.

This dramatic example of the House pattern is made with dark blue fabric set against a white background. The red chimneys atop each house add a necessary spark of strong color that is effectively repeated in the narrow binding. The strong design of the quilt is enhanced both by the blue and white "planks" of the border and by the handsome quilting in the white blocks.

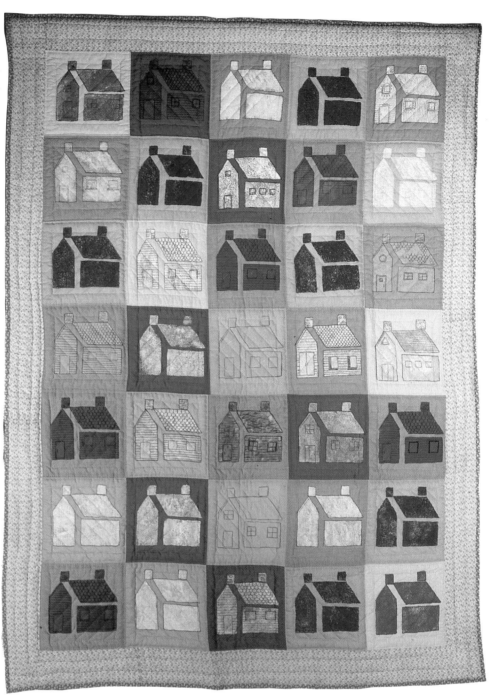

60. *House Quilt*, 87″ x 67″, made in 1985 by Elizabeth Miller, Chauncey, Ohio. Photograph copyright by John Sattler.

HOUSE: CONTEMPORARY

The traditional House or Schoolhouse pattern has been charmingly updated in this quilt by Elizabeth Miller. Each house has been stenciled with acrylic paints, a change from the usual pieced blocks. The primary colors set against white and pastel backgrounds make a colorful statement. In some of the blocks, simple outline embroidery provides added eye appeal to the overall design. Hand quilting in the blocks and in the border has been used sparingly so as not to distract from the individual houses. Elizabeth's *House Quilt* and her *Crazy Quilt* on page 59 show how the imaginative application of paint to fabric can contribute effectively to an artistic whole, as a viable substitute for traditional pieced or appliquéd patterns.

Quilting and Twentieth-Century Ideas

Quiltmakers today seem to be divided into two distinct groups: those that make quilts based on patterns handed down by quiltmakers through several generations, and those that use the quilt as a medium for contemporary self-expression and focus primarily on creating an original design. From time to time, quiltmakers bridge the gap between traditional and original designs by combining elements of both in their work, as you have seen in the quilts illustrated here.

As more and more artists have used the quilt as their canvas, traditional quiltmakers have watched with apprehension, and question the direction that quilts are taking now. Their concern seems to be about the preservation of fine quilting skills. Will standards of quiltmaking remain as important as they once were, or will the technical aspects of the craft be lost as more emphasis is given to originality of design?

At the same time, contemporary fiber artists wonder why so many quiltmakers are leery of flexing their creative muscles beyond the fine reproduction of traditional patterns, and why *process* of quilting is considered more essential than aesthetic originality. Thus, the fiber artists believe that if you are going to spend a thousand hours meticulously stitching a quilt, it is far better for it to be a vehicle of your own originality rather than another fine version of a design seen a thousand times over.

As I began to study contemporary quilts and talk to the artists creating the work, I became more and more aware of the gulf that separates traditional quiltmakers and fiber artists. In discussing these matters with one of the artists, I heard the following.

ELAINE PLOGMAN: "I feel that by far the most important aspect of quiltmaking today is design. There are so many sources of excellent information on quiltmaking technique in the form of books, magazines, workshops, and even television that the average quiltmaker with a few years of experience is capable of executing a technically fine piece of work. I wonder when some of the large and 'important' quilt shows are going to stop bestowing awards principally on the basis of how finely a piece is quilted and a corner mitered. I think it is a 'cop-out' on the part of the judges in that they can justify their decision on how well a quilt meets their list of requirements for an award winner. We are turning ourselves into quilting machines when we place more (or even as much) value upon the quality of the work than on the design of the work. The work of the hand is valued more than the work of the brain. Don't get me wrong; I have been known to remove the binding from a piece repeatedly to even up an edge until it meets my standards. I certainly believe that a quilt that is sloppily made should be disqualified from a show; but I do think

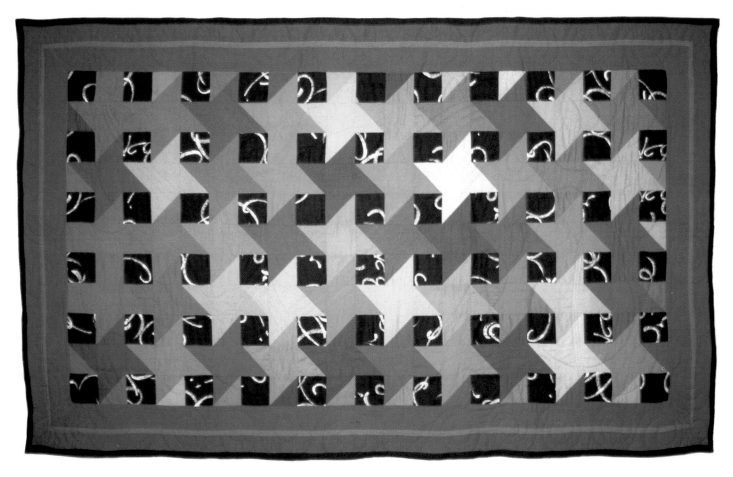

61. *Milky Way*, 44″ x 74″, made in 1986 by Lois Tamir, Dallas, Texas. The solid colors of the *Milky Way* shine brightly against the dark background, in which the white swirls provide a fascinating sense of depth. Completed very close to the deadline for this book, Lois's piece is published here for the first time and has only been on exhibition over her living-room couch. Photograph courtesy the artist.

that criteria for judging quilts are due for a major revision."

Pat Morris, well known for her scrupulous judging at major quilting events across the United States and for her regular columns in several publications, shared her feelings on the subject.

PAT MORRIS:"The design versus technique debate has been raging in quiltmaking for as long as I have been active in the field. Both sides in this debate have valid points to make. From my point of view, I feel the debate is foolish: both design and technique need to work together to produce a good example of the quiltmaker's art.

"The lackluster, uninspiring, traditional quilt brilliantly executed makes me wonder what heights this quiltmaker might have attained had imagination been brought into play with as much skill as fingers. Just so, a dismally executed quilt of innovative design makes me wonder what might have been had the quiltmaker brought some technical expertise into the picture along with imagination.

"It seems obvious to me that many quiltmakers need to hang on to their technical skills while expanding their design horizons, and that many other quiltmakers need to master the basic skills to meld with their innovative design ideas.

"None of the famous couturiers such as Chanel, Dior, and Balenciaga, whose designs have sparked the public imagination, changed the fashion trends of millions, and passed into legend, would have lasted one season if these beautifully designed garments had hung cockeyed on the customer, with drooping hems, zippers that didn't mesh, and seams that didn't meet.

"If an item is shabbily executed, it does not merit serious consideration by the viewer, no matter what the field is, and this is as true in quiltmaking as elsewhere. By the same token, mediocre design on which great technical skill has been lavished deserves no more than a 'ho-hum' in passing.

"Both sides of the design versus technique debate need to move closer together as the technical expert expands design horizons and the design expert improves workmanship."

Let us compare quiltmaking to other forms of art. Consider the woodworker. We have two varieties: the hobbyist and the studio woodcraftsman. The first type, who may spend one to four hours a week woodworking as a method of relaxation, often works in pine because of its affordability. Pine is easy to work with and sells well in the country crafts market, should the woodworker attempt to sell his works. Prices can be kept low because the furniture is sometimes made without regard to such time-consuming techniques as dovetailing, mitering, pegging, proper finishing, and so forth.

A skilled woodcraftsman can be found by inspecting the small details of his work. How does he joint boards: are they simply machine-butted or have they been intricately hand-cut, mortised, and tenoned? Has he used a countersunk screw to hold a board in place, or has he taken the time to peg and wedge a joint properly?

When an art instructor takes a class of freshmen through the basics of any art medium, he instructs them in the proper procedures for that art. A ceramics class is first shown how to prepare their clay for the wheel. If not done properly, the clay may explode once it is heated in the kiln. A painting class is guided in the preparation of their materials: brushes must be treated with respect, canvas must be stretched before use. A weaving class is shown the ropes (no pun intended) of warping a loom. There are some basic rules of the road one must follow no matter what field is chosen.

Many recent quilt contests and exhibitions have featured unique items such as quilted kites suspended from the ceiling, quilted kimonos large enough to fit three people, quilted animals, and quilted mobiles with tattered strands of fabric wafting in the breeze. Paper quilts have emerged and been exhibited alongside "normal" fabric quilts. *Webster's New World Dictionary* (1970 edition) defines a quilt as "a bedcover made of two layers of cloth filled with down, cotton, wool, etc., and stitched together in lines or patterns to keep the filling in place," and "anything quilted or like a quilt." Perhaps today's standards are too freely stretching the word *like* in this definition. With the constant changes quilting is going through, perhaps traditional quilters would be more comfortable if someone were to redefine the word *quilt*.

The artists who created the contemporary quilts featured in this book were asked several questions relating to the quilt world—past, present, and future.

Which do you feel is the most important aspect of quiltmaking today—design, technique, workmanship, et cetera?

MARLENE ANDREY: "A really great quilt is good in all aspects of quiltmaking—design, technique, and workmanship. I don't think microscopic quilting stitches automatically make a prize-winning quilt, but I don't like to see a good design ruined by poor or sloppy workmanship."

BARBARA CARON: "I cannot see past bad workmanship in a quilt. If one chooses quiltmaking as a medium, I think it is important to learn the skills so that workmanship contributes to the design rather than detracting from it."

NELL COGSWELL: "For me, design is the most important aspect of quiltmaking. Every time I think I've seen *everything*, something new turns up. It's great!"

NANCY DICE: "For contemporary quiltmakers, the hardest thing to do is to develop a style of one's own—to resist the temptation to turn that workshop project into a carbon copy of the teacher's style and instead to use the ideas and techniques in an expression of individual style. This tendency is, unfortunately, perpetuated by show jurors who will accept and reward 'copies.'

"Another problem is craftsmanship: with the common use of 'quickie' techniques and the emphasis on finishing projects as fast as possible, or producing large quantities of work, has come a regrettable sloppiness in attention to details. Again, many jurors for 'art' shows seem to accept sloppy work—probably because they haven't been trained as quilters."

JEAN EITEL: "It is distressing to me that some contemporary quilt artists have adopted the attitude that art quilts do not require the same excellence in workmanship that traditional quilts require. If the artist were enrolled in a fine-arts program that included a subject such as printmaking, that attitude would not be accepted by an instructor or judge in an art show. The same should apply to quiltmaking. Standards should never be sacrificed for a trendy image."

LIL GOLSTON: "I would have to choose workmanship as the most important aspect of quiltmaking. On the bus on the way home from The Great American Quilt Festival in New York (1986), the most frequently heard

62. *Medallion Wall Hanging*, 31″ x 28″, made in 1986 by Tammy Porath, Troy, Michigan. The focal point of the medallion is a single Eight-Pointed Star. This traditional design has been updated by the use of striped and patterned fabrics in unusual ways. As she was marking each template on her fabric, Tammy took great care to place all eight diamonds of the Star in the same position on the fabric pattern. The result is an artwork of great charm and appeal. Photograph by E. Rousseau.

63. *Reverse Appliqué Banner*, 30″ x 48″. Made in 1982 by Barbara Rickey, the quilt features an assortment of patterns by Charlotte Patera and Mexican folk art symbols that have been drafted by the artist.

comments were about the poor workmanship spoiling otherwise beautiful designs. Quiltmaking is a *craft*. Today, as fifty years ago, guidelines for judged shows are heavily weighted toward workmanship. A plain Nine Patch, beautifully executed, will still bring blue ribbons."

PAM JOHNSON: "I think the most interesting aspect of quiltmaking today is not how a quilt is made (technique, workmanship, design, et cetera) but *why* a quilt is made. None of us needs quilts in the sense that warm, economical bedcovers were once needed. Each of us has her own reason for making a quilt: to comfort a loved one, to win thousands of dollars in prize money, to express oneself as an artist, or perhaps simply to pass the time. This variety of purpose results in vast differences in how each quilt will look in terms of design, technique, and workmanship.

"A certain amount of tension exists between 'contemporary' and 'traditional' quiltmakers. Perhaps if we could keep in mind the many different reasons for making quilts, we could go further toward understanding the great diversity of forms they take."

BARBARA RICKEY: "Design is the most important. If the design is not good, it doesn't really matter how fabulous the workmanship is. Of course, good workmanship is to be expected, but almost anyone can learn acceptable skills. Poor workmanship can spoil an otherwise good design, but if the design isn't there to begin with, there is really very little to hold one's attention."

ANN RHODE: "If the total image is effective, I don't care if all points meet or if there are twelve stitches to the inch."

AMI SIMMS: "I strive for an even balance between

workmanship and design. One without the other is a waste of effort."

NANCY SMELTZER: "All of the elements are important if the composition is to work. I hate pieces that are technically correct, but the composition is boring. I do feel, however, that there is more to art than whether the straight of the grain is lined up correctly on every appliqué piece, and whether or not the stitches on the back are as even as on the front."

How do you think quilting has changed over the last fifty years?

MARLENE ANDREY: "I think the main way quilting has changed is that quilters are willing to experiment and take chances with many different designs, techniques, and mediums. I've seen quilts that were made of paper and stuffed brassieres!"

BARBARA CARON: "I believe that there have always been quiltmakers who found the process creatively rewarding as well as practical and functional. However, I think that today there are more quiltmakers whose primary motivator is the potential for creativity. I see this verified by all of the small wall quilts we make and see. Many of these quilts are too small to serve any other function except decoration. I know that my greatest pleasure in quiltmaking is the ability to produce something that is visually pleasing to me."

MARGERY COSGROVE: "The artist has become emphasized over the craftsman. The personal view, statement, the pictorial element is more important."

PAT COX: "One change from the thirties to the seventies and eighties has been from scrap to art. . . ."

NANCY DICE: "Quilters today are exposed to far more outside influences than in the past; this is as true in quilting and other crafts as it is in national affairs. Magazines, books, TV, and the availability of workshops, formal instruction in schools, and the wide dissemination of the ideas and techniques of influential teachers have brought quilting to more and more people. This has been good and bad: good, because more people have known the joy of making something beautiful; bad, because so many people seem to be satisfied with easy and quick solutions, or with producing a copy of someone else's work."

FLAVIN GLOVER: "More available tools, publications, fabric selection is greater, increased leisure time, more exposure and attention given to handmade quilts."

LIL GOLSTON: "Essentially, I don't think it's really changed all that much. Blankets were widely available fifty years ago, so quilting for warmth wasn't a woman's main concern (for the most part). I believe women then, as now, used their quilts as a creative outlet, and changes in the way quilts look is simply a natural growth of the art form."

PAMELA JOHNSON: "When I think of the 1930s, certain quilt patterns come to mind: Grandmother's Flower Garden, Dresden Plate, and Double Wedding Ring. Within each pattern type, so many of those quilts were virtually identical. Were all those *quiltmakers* virtually identical as well? What caused this mass conformity, this lack of innovation?

"I delight in the fact that over the past fifteen years or so, for some quiltmakers, quiltmaking has again become what it once was: a reflection of the people who make them *and* the times in which they are being made. Instead of being mired in the past (though certainly much has been learned from it) the contemporary quiltmaker departs from convention to offer an individual vision."

SUSAN LOCHER: "In many areas, I don't think it has changed much at all. There seems to be a lot of interest among younger people now, while I remember when I was a teenager, we thought of quilting as a nice thing, but certainly nothing we wanted to do."

ANN RHODE: "Technology—computers, Xerox, et cetera, have helped today's quilters with designing."

AMI SIMMS: "Quilters have become more sophisticated. With readily available and continually growing quilt media, our horizons have been expanded and our minds challenged. Anything goes nowadays. Quilting, now more than ever before, can satisfy almost *any* creative urge."

As I did the research for this book, hundreds of slides and photographs of contemporary quilts were sent to me from quilters all across America. Every quilting book I could get my hands on was read several times, and I attended as many exhibitions as I could get to. It soon became apparent that elements of traditional patterns and techniques are evident in the work of even the most contemporary quiltmakers. A look at the work of Michael James, a well-known contemporary quilt artist, shows hints of traditional influences in many of his works. In his book *The Second Quiltmaker's Handbook*, images of the Drunkard's Path pattern are seen in his quilt *Aurora* (plate 10); a traditional Log Cabin has been changed into a delightful *Poppies* in plate 13, and traces of the Pineapple technique (a technique similar in construction to the Log Cabin) are seen in his quilt *Winter Cactus* (plate 32).

There is no doubt that quilting styles will change in the years to come, just as clothing styles have changed time and time again.

Every few years, a new fashion trend comes into being; some people accept the change, some don't. However, there are some articles of clothing that never seem to go out of style. Basic black pumps, the tailored trench coat, a dark navy A-line skirt and a white tailored blouse look as proper today as they did twenty years ago. Whoever thought saddle shoes or miniskirts would come back into style when we packed them away in the fifties and sixties? I believe that the traditions of fine quiltmaking will certainly remain important throughout the current changes, and that they will always be respected for being the axis around which the art of quilting has revolved.

Collecting Contemporary Quilts

Quilts from America's past are a treasured find nowadays. A quilt that is in good condition, and free from stain and signs of neglect, can sometimes bring a hefty sum to the owner. Great-grandmother's fancywork can often be found hanging on the walls of leading museums and art galleries across the country. As a result of the tremendous popularity of the "country look," collectors have been searching through garage sales, estate sales, and antiques shops for primitive pine furniture, old crockery, tinware, teddy bears, pewter, and old quilts. Most individuals who are tuned in to the "old-is-better" theme know what to look for in an antique quilt to which they have been attracted by the color and design: original binding; hand-carded cotton batting (you can see the seeds through the fabric if you hold the quilt up to the light); precision in piecing and appliqué; and tiny, even stitches. And if the quilt also has the signature of the maker and a date, so much the better. These all add to the value of an antique quilt. But what should the collector look for in a *new* quilt? What elements of workmanship and pattern will assure the buyer that he or she is making a good investment?

Quilts can be used to add a colorful geometric statement to the clean lines of modern furnishings, and often at a price lower than what you would expect to pay for a fine work of art. These new quilts will also, in time, be considered worthy antiques if well preserved. Today,

with more and more fiber artists creating contemporary quilts, it can be hard to decide what is and what is not a good buy.

Many of the factors used to determine the value of an antique quilt hold true in deciding the value of a new example of quilt art. Mitered corners, while not obligatory, are considered superior to corners that are butted. A narrow binding, also with miters, is preferable to a wide binding unless the quilt is a modern

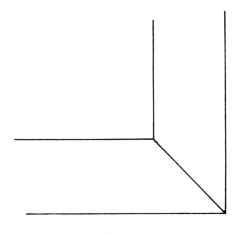

Mitered Corner

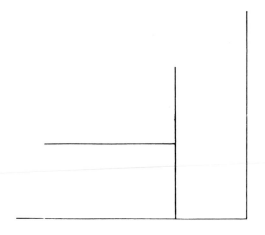

Butted Square Corner

interpretation of an old Amish quilt, for Amish quilts often had one-inch bindings. The binding should be well filled with batting and should not wobble around the quilt. Tiny stitches in a pattern that enhances the overall design of the quilt again are preferable, but larger stitches will suffice if done very evenly. Pencil lines used to mark the quilting design should not be seen on the face of the quilt.

On the reverse side of the quilt, the color of the backing should be in keeping with the color on the front. If the backing of the quilt is seamed, two evenly spaced seams are better than a center seam. If one seam has been used, it should run from top to bottom, not through the center of the quilt.

Above all the quilt should be pleasing and stimulating to the eye: colors should blend together well, and the blocks should be consistently pieced of the same fabric (a slight color change or variation in the printed fabrics in one or two blocks may indicate that the quilter ran out of fabric and had to "make do"). Lattice strips (the sashing that runs between pieced or appliquéd blocks) should always run in straight lines; they should not dip to fit the uneven piecing of a block.

One should note, however, that the above recommendations are not cast in concrete for contemporary quilts. Many "art" quilts being produced today are not made in rectangular or square shapes, for example, the circular mandala quilts made popular by Katie Pasquini of California. Some quilts may contain a wavy border to accentuate a theme or mood. Quilting motifs may intentionally strongly oppose the designs of the quilt. These factors should be taken into account when inspecting a quilt for purchase.

As so many quilts are being produced today, it would be foolish to try to predict what patterns and designs will be popular fifty years from now. One can safely assume that any *original* design that is pleasing to the eye would probably prove to be a good investment. Patterns such as Grandmother's Flower Garden, Nine Patch, and Trip Around the World are old classics, so they could never be considered unusual, but this does *not* mean that you should not buy a quilt in these patterns if you find them very appealing!

Today's collectors are delighted when they discover an antique pictorial quilt, a true "folk art quilt." Quilts of this nature can be very expensive if and when you can find them. A pictorial quilt is best described as "an original artistic design thought up, sewn and quilted into a form that either tells a story, shows a picture, or convinces the viewer to believe that the quilt represents a specific image" (see *America's Pictorial Quilts,* 1985, by Caron L. Mosey). Pictorial quilts can tell us something about the quilter: what she likes and dislikes; what was important to her when she made the quilt. Fifty or even one hundred years from now contemporary pictorial quilts will help to tell others about the life-styles of the 1980s. Also, in the future, it will be possible for quilt historians to date contemporary to the 1975–1985 period, in the same way that Crazy quilts can be dated to the last quarter of the nineteenth century. Over the last few years, finely stitched delicate appliqué has been the rage in traditional quilting circles while quilts featuring abstract designs, or fiber art, are being produced by contemporary artists, who are adding another important look to the ever-growing repertory of quiltmaking styles. A fine example

Two seams, evenly spaced, are preferred

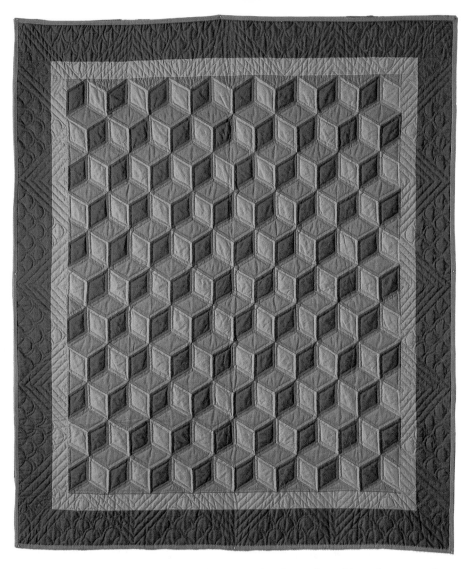

64. Tumbling Blocks, 48″ x 41″. Made in 1986 by the author, this quilt was made to resemble old Amish quilts. Hand-pieced and hand-quilted. The quilting motif in the borders was adapted from an antique Amish quilt, and features small clam shells set in pyramidal fashion. Photograph by Schecter Lee.

of any quilt such as these would make a worthy addition to any collection.

The cost of acquiring a quilt will vary according to the prominence of the artists who create them. Beginning quiltmakers will understandably charge quite low prices, while "brand-name" quilters, that is, quilters who have made a name for themselves in today's quilting and art circles, can command unusually high prices for their work. Some quilts are priced according to the number of hours required to make the piece, while others are priced by the square foot ($75.00 per square foot is not unheard of!). Just as with collectibles of any type, pieces made by well-known artists are worth special consideration for investment. Quilters such as Michael James, Nancy Crow, Jinny Beyer, Judy Mathieson, Katie Pasquini, and many others produce very unusual, and very original contemporary quilts ranging in size from small hangings to bed-size pieces. If you are on the hunt for a quilt from a "name" quilter, the same standards of excellence should apply. Make sure that what you are getting is worth the price you will be paying.

If you are not sure about the value of the quilt, it might be worth consulting an experienced quilt collector or a licensed quilt appraiser. Don't trust the judgment of a general estate appraiser unless he can prove he knows one end of a quilt from another.

65. *New Crayons*, 57″ x 41″, copyright 1986 by Nancy Dice. This quilt, a companion piece to *Bird Wars: The Origin of Super Goose* (see p.29), simulates a page taken from a coloring book. The three-dimensional crayon box in brilliant solid colors has been tossed onto the page. An aqua crayon is being tried out, but whoever is doing the coloring is not staying inside the lines! The gray and white drawing of the One Patch quilt contains curved lines so that it simulates a drawing. The words *new crayons* have been repeatedly quilted into the background of the "page." Nancy claims that "this comes from a remembrance of my fourth-grade teacher, Miss Leckie, who entered class on the first day of school and wrote her name in big beautiful cursive writing on the board. *New Crayons* is written as beautifully as I can manage!" Photograph courtesy the artist.

66. *Renaissance*, 48″ x 50″, copyright 1981 by Elaine Plogman. Owned by Cincinnati Bell, *Renaissance* contains two easily recognizable traditional quilt patterns, Grandmother's Fan and Hosanna. The Hosanna blocks are the focal point of the quilt, centered in warm orange and gold colors. The quilt is machine-pieced and hand-quilted, and uses cottons, blends, and some satin and velvet upholstery fabric. The well-balanced use of both curved and straight segments makes this quilt interesting and captivating. Photograph courtesy the artist.

Newspaper clippings and magazine articles (should there be any) about the quilt you are buying will add to its value if preserved with the quilt. The more ribbons and awards a quilt has won, and the number of times it has been published, can raise the price of a quilt considerably. These items will be like a quilt diary to a future owner of the quilt, and the more information you have about it, the better off you are. Photographs of the quiltmaker alone and/or with the quilt and photographs of the quilt on display in public exhibitions are important additions to the history of the quilt.

The final factor in buying a quilt is probably the most obvious. Above all, *like* the quilt you want to buy. Purchasing a quilt for status or for strictly investment purposes is like keeping a large diamond in your safety deposit box. It does no good to keep it hidden, and it will do you no good if you can't enjoy it. Quilts are made to be caressed; they are meant to be seen and used. They are flexible pieces of art that are meant to be enjoyed now as well as in the future. After all, what other collectible or artwork can be found hanging on a wall, covering a bed, draping over a couch, and keeping you warm on a cold winter night?

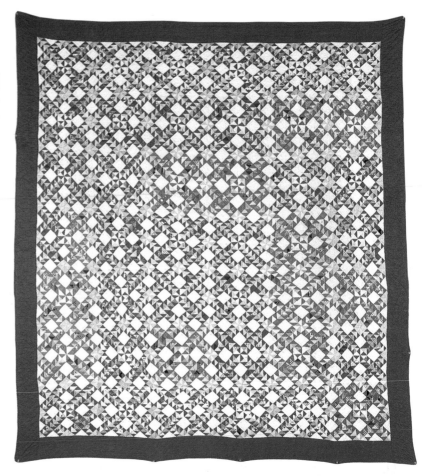

67. Wild Goose Chase, 88″ x 80″, c. 1920, maker unknown. Quilt courtesy Ron and Kathy Hind, Hickory Hill Antiques, Redmond, Washington. Photograph by E. Rousseau.

68. *Barely Enough Take 2*, 43″ x 43″, copyright 1983 by Ann Rhode. Ann has successfully combined a traditional star pattern with a variation of the ever-popular Log Cabin. The manner in which the star blocks have been set forms a pleasing Medallion effect. Photograph courtesy the artist.

The Patterns

The patterns that follow are basic single-block patterns that can be used to create a quilt with a very traditional or contemporary appearance, depending on your choice of fabric and setting. Because today's quiltmakers are adapting patterns to fit their own needs, yardage requirements or finished quilt size have not been provided. Both measurements are dependent upon the number of blocks, setting (diagonal or straight), and width of lattice strips used, if any. In addition, it is important to mention that most of the contemporary quilts featured in this book are original designs created by the individual artists. Many of these contemporary quilts are *copyrighted designs,* and by law, may not be duplicated. With the wide range of published patterns available to today's quiltmaker and the large number of quilting books and magazines that feature photographs of exciting quilts, it should not be hard for even the beginning quiltmaker to select a pattern and turn it into an attractive quilt.

Because of the large number of excellent books covering the basics of quiltmaking, *Contemporary Quilts from Traditional Designs* will not attempt to cover this subject. If you are new to quiltmaking, I strongly recommend any of the following books as good, all-around introductions to the world of quilting: *The Standard Book of Quiltmaking and Collecting* by Marguerite Ickis; *You Can Be a Super Quilter!* by Carla Hassel; *Super Quilter II* by Carla Hassel; *It's OK to Sit on My Quilt Book* by Mary Ellen Hopkins.

Once you feel confident about your basic quiltmaking skills, it is quite easy (and fun!) to create your own designs based on traditional patterns. There is no limit to the number of variations that can be made using a single pattern as a grid. The use of color, with either solid or printed fabrics, is only one tool with which to work. Mixing two or more traditional patterns can create new designs, and these designs in turn can be changed accordingly. For a good example, look carefully at the three quilts drafted in diagrams A, B, and C. Each quilt is based on two patterns: Jacob's Ladder and St. Louis Star. Diagram A shows how the points at the outer edge of each block join together to give a sense of continuity to the whole. In diagram B, the addition of a checkerboard pattern to the St. Louis Star block in the center provides an extra "oomph" and seems to complete the design by filling in the open areas. However, if the checkerboard areas are deleted from the center portion of the quilt, as in diagram C, the resulting large open area provides ample room for elaborate quilting designs.

The number of designs that can be created by the combination of two or more traditional blocks is endless. Thousands of patterns and pattern variations are available in quilting books and magazines. But how do you go about successfully combining two blocks? The easiest

Diagram A

Diagram B

Diagram C

method, and the one that I prefer using with my beginning design students, is to experiment with patterns of a similar type. In this instance, *type* refers to block division: Four Patch, Six Patch, Nine Patch, and so forth (see diagram D). As you compare blocks of similar divisions, pay close attention to the point at which various elements of each block touch the outside edges. Referring back to diagram A, observe how the points of the Jacob's Ladder and St. Louis Star blocks come together. Because each block is based on a Nine Patch division, and because the points are able to connect at an exact point, these two patterns work well together.

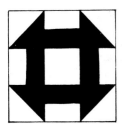

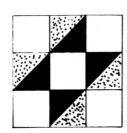

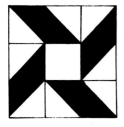

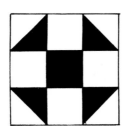

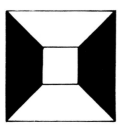

Diagram D Nine Patch Blocks

It is possible to combine blocks without regard to block division. Many contemporary quilts shown on previous pages are good examples. *Reflections on Arnheim* (p. 2), *Barely Enough Take 2* (p. 74), *Social Interaction* (p. 55), and *From the Woods to the Water* (p. 9) all successfully combine two or more traditional blocks. The key to accomplishing this is to have patience and "play" with a sketch pad or, more to the point, with lots of graph paper.

Several of the quilts you have seen earlier in the book are based on a single traditional pattern. Instead of repeating the blocks throughout the work, the quiltmakers have taken liberties with the various shapes in the blocks and rearranged them to form alternative designs. A good example of this is the quilt shown here titled *They Never Told Me There'd Be Days Like This!* Nell Cogswell has used the traditional Farmer's Daughter block around the perimeter of the quilt, making it appear at first glance to be a traditional scrap quilt. But a closer look at the center portion of the quilt reveals that the blocks seem to disintegrate into chaos. Nell could not have selected a better title for her quilt!

Color changes throughout an otherwise "normal" quilt can give a fresh, contemporary appearance. *Washed Out to See* (p. 39), *October Landscape* (p. 5), and *Passages* (p. 41) are all prime examples of the effectiveness of careful color selection.

Gradual changes in the size of the block, or in the individual templates used to make the block, are also wonderful methods of altering a traditional pattern. *Monkey Wrench I* by Pamela Gustavson Johnson (p. 33) is an impressive example of her skill at the drafting board. From itty-bitty "wrenches" in the center of the piece to very large examples near the borders, *Monkey Wrench I* has a strong three-dimensional image. *Chubby Checkers* (p. 51) and *Storm at Sea Yellow Square II* (p. 35) have both been designed using gradual enlarging or stretching techniques. The process for creating this sort of optical illusion is easier than you would think. Diagram E shows a simple Variable Star block being "stretched" on graph paper. Another method of "stretching" a block is by experimenting with plastic wrap or a large balloon. (No, you didn't read that wrong!) Using a ball-point pen, draft the block directly on the plastic or balloon. Once this is done, take the drawing to a copy machine. Lay the drawing on the copy machine and, with your fingers (and maybe a friend's fingers too!), stretch the plastic or balloon and push the start button on the machine. The machine will pick up the ink on the plastic and an image of your fingers; ignore the fingers and concentrate on the design. As long as you are at the copy machine, make several different copies stretching the block in various directions. When you get a design that appeals to you, enlarge the copy of it either on a copy machine that has

69. *They Never Told Me There'd Be Days Like This!* 70″ x 50½″, made in 1985 by Nell Cogswell, Carlisle, Massachusetts. Based on the traditional Farmer's Daughter pattern.

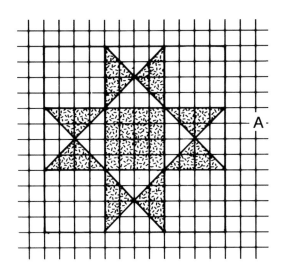

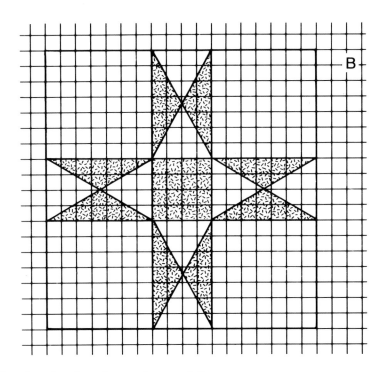

Diagram E Variable Star showing how to create a variation

enlarging capabilities, or at home using the grid system of enlargement. Who said experimenting was only for scientists?

Because there are so many ways to create a contemporary quilt, it is impossible to provide you with step-by-step instructions. If the quilts in *Contemporary Quilts from Traditional Designs* catch your fancy, pick your favorite traditional block and set aside a "play day." See what different designs you can create based on the patterns given you by our ancestors, the true pioneers of fiber art. The following are but a few of the patterns used in the traditional quilts found in this book. Many other patterns are available in countless quilting publications. I hope by comparing the old to the new you will acquire an increased appreciation for all styles of quiltmaking. We can still appreciate and continue to produce traditional quilts similar to those made a hundred years ago. At the same time, we can also create new quilts that will represent the talents of quiltmakers working in the late 1900s.

NOTE: The patterns that follow show two outlines for each template. The innermost line is the sewing line; the outer line is the cutting line.

TUMBLING BLOCKS

The Tumbling Blocks pattern uses a single template, A. Two sizes are provided for you to choose from. To obtain the three-dimensional effect, it is necessary to sew the patches so that the darkest triangle is always placed in the same position (see diagram above).

For each block, cut three diamonds:

1 dark, 1 medium, 1 light

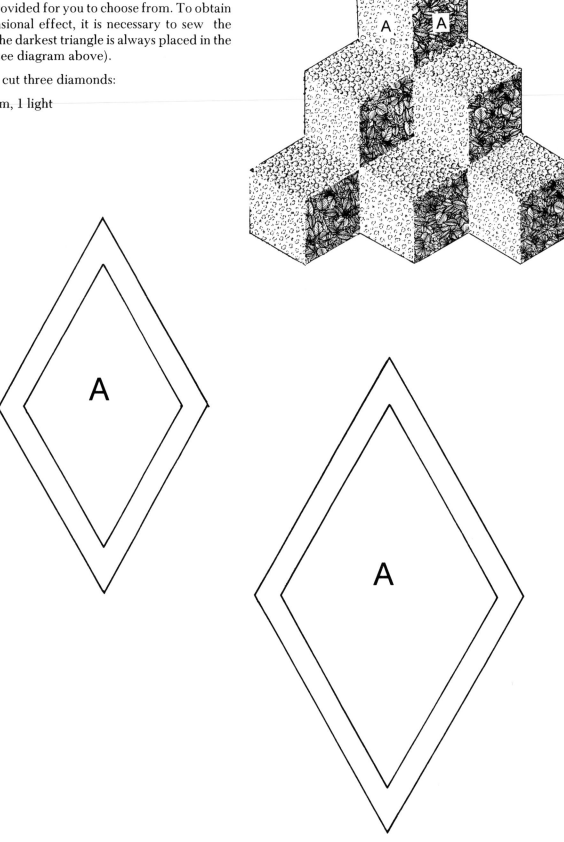

GRANDMOTHER'S FAN

7-inch-square block

The Grandmother's Fan block can be made in either of two ways: all pieced, or using a combination of piecing and appliqué. If the latter method is chosen, the "fans" in the block are pieced together, and the curved sections are appliquéd on.

For each block, cut:

1 of template A in a print or solid
4 of template B in various colors or prints
1 of template C in white, muslin, or light solid

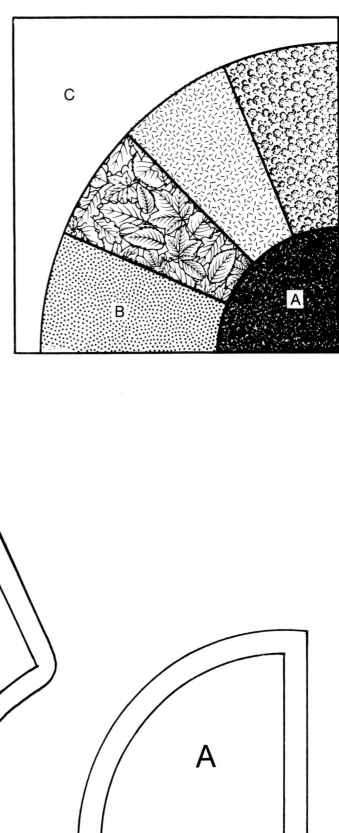

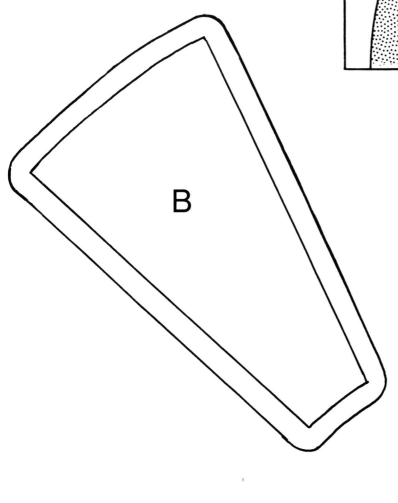

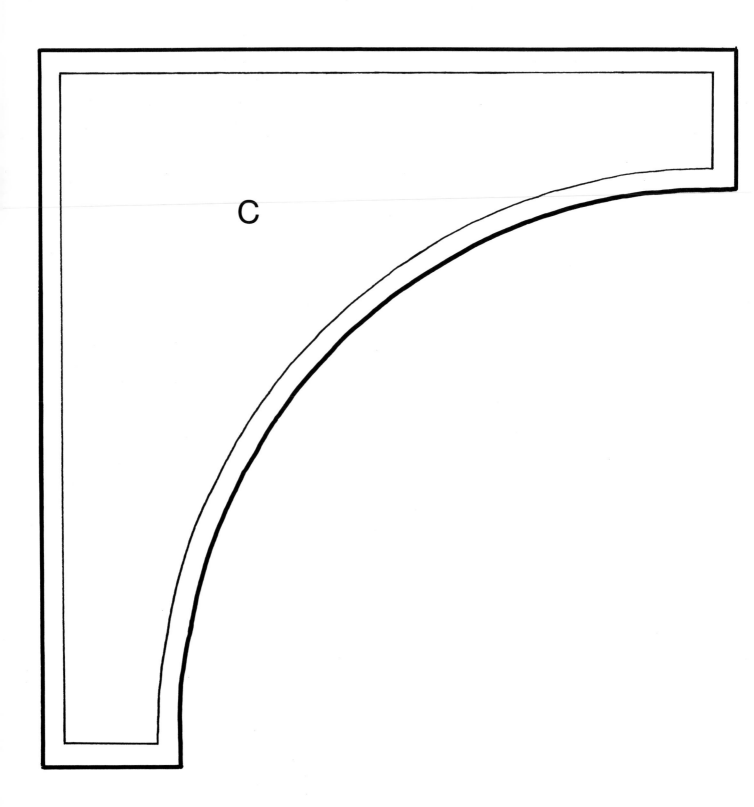

C

PINWHEEL

4-inch square or 6-inch square block

A single triangle is all that is required to piece together the Pinwheel block. Two sizes are provided for you to choose from. Careful handling along the bias edge of the triangles will prevent distortion. This pattern makes an effective bold statement when two colors are used throughout the quilt, and it is equally charming when used as a scrap-bag pattern.

For each block, cut:

4 of template A in a light color or print
4 of template A in a dark color or print

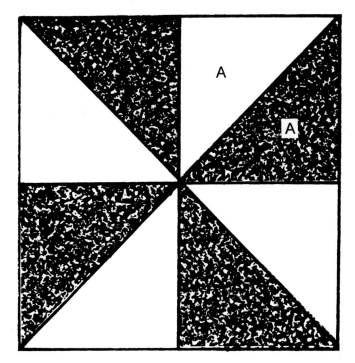

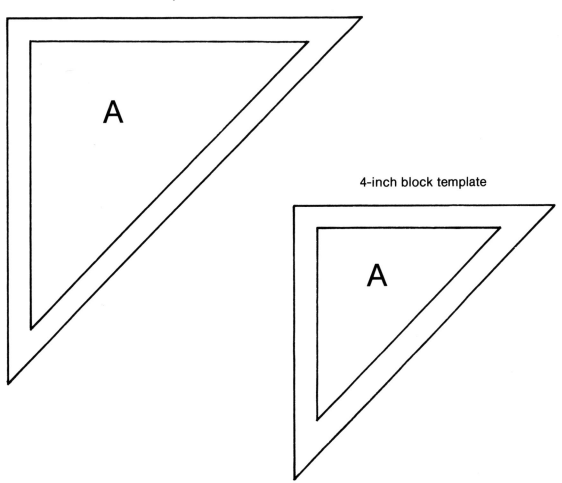

6-inch block template

A

4-inch block template

A

STORM AT SEA

Storm at Sea may be made with either two or three colors. The guidelines shown below apply to the use of three selected fabrics. The diagram at the right shows a block as it would appear in a single setting, perhaps as a pillow top or tote bag. When the pattern is used to create an entire quilt, assembly follows an alternate row arrangement: row one, row two, row one, row two, and so forth (see diagram F).

For one block, cut:

16 of template A in a dark print or solid
16 of template B in a light print or solid
4 of template C in a medium print or solid
8 of template D in a light print or solid
8 of template D *reversed* in a light print or solid
4 of template E in a dark print or solid
4 of template F in a medium print or solid
4 of template G in a light print or solid
1 of template H in a medium print or solid

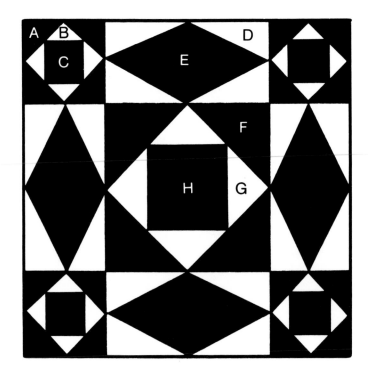

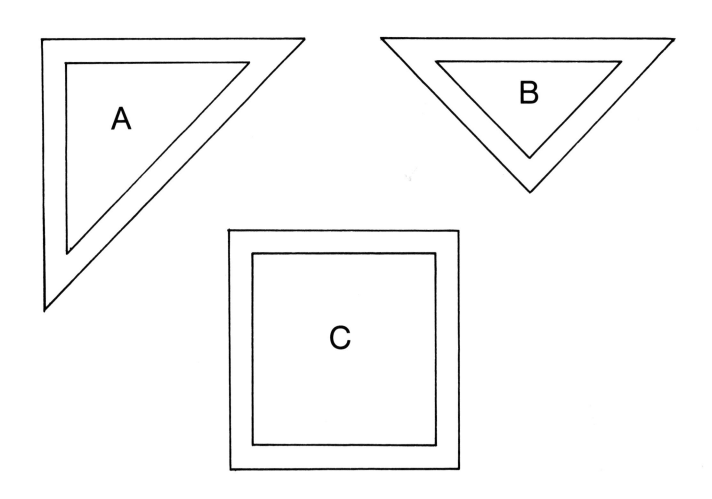

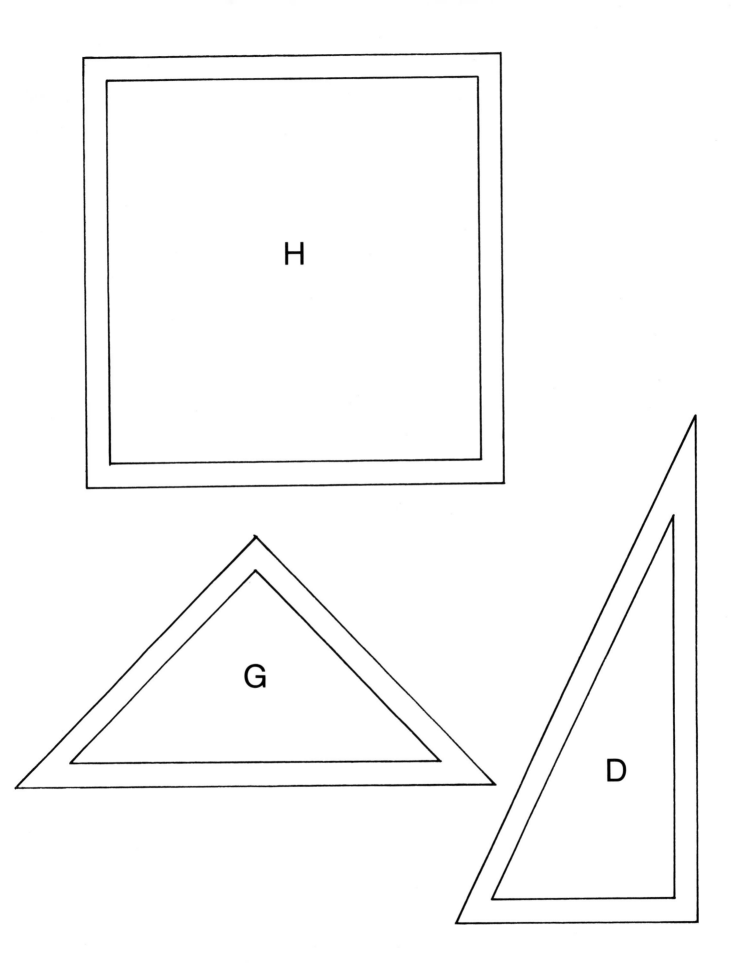

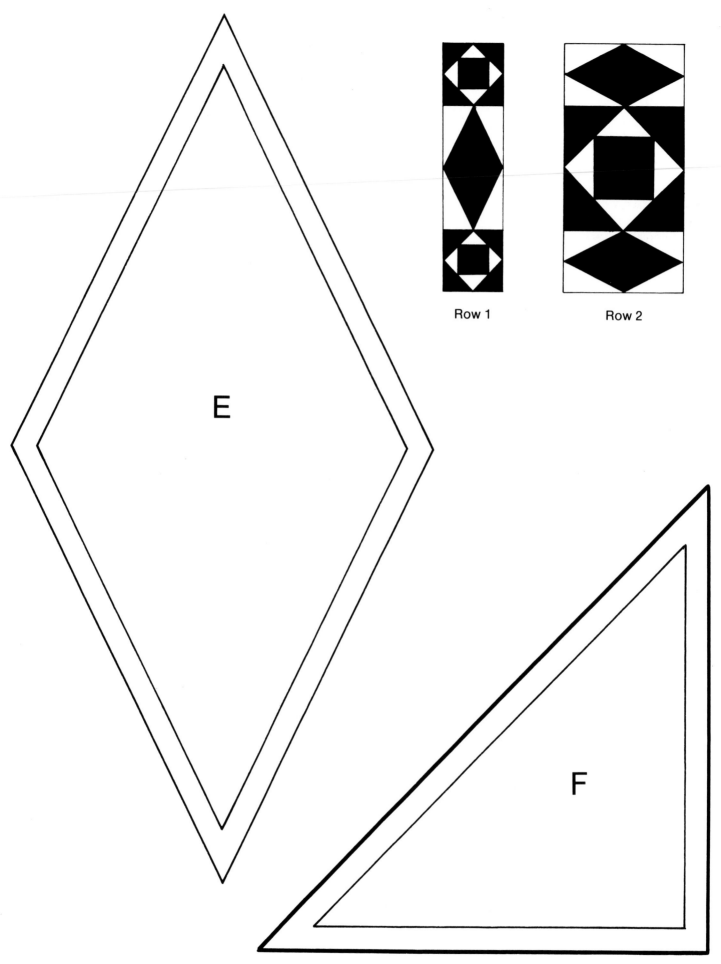

Row 1

Row 2

E

F

MONKEY WRENCH

12-inch-square block

The Monkey Wrench pattern is most effective when two colors are used throughout the entire quilt. It is an easy block to piece, following a Nine Patch arrangement.

For each block, cut:

8 of template A light
8 of template A dark
4 of template B light
4 of template B dark
1 of template C light

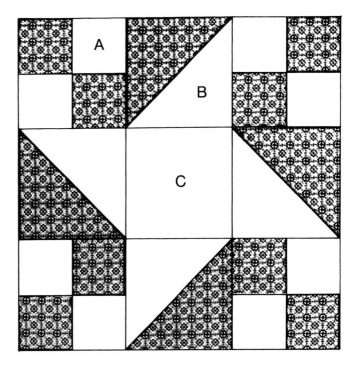

12" block

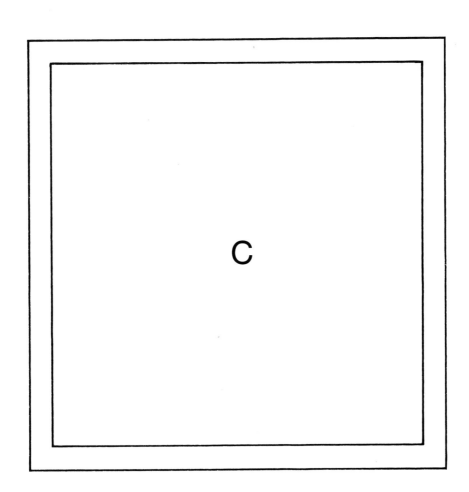

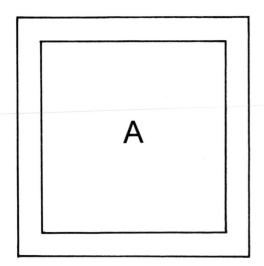

A

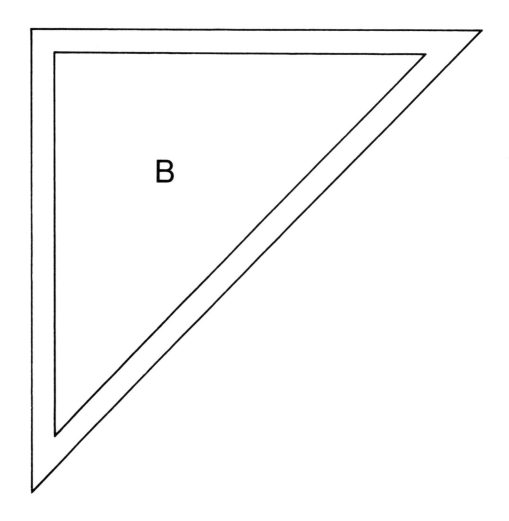

B

PINE TREE

18-inch-square block

Even with the large number of pieces required to make the Pine Tree block, it is a fairly easy block to assemble if careful attention is given to the bias edges in the triangles.

For each block, cut:

3 of template A light
36 of template B dark
30 of template B light
2 of template C light
1 of template D medium
1 of template E medium
1 of template F light
1 of template F *reversed*, light
1 of template G medium

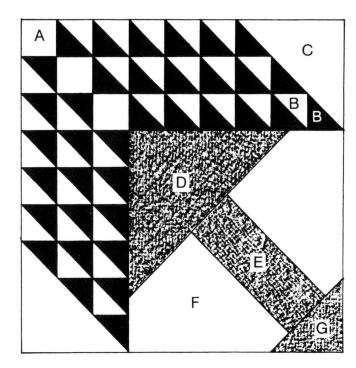

18″ block

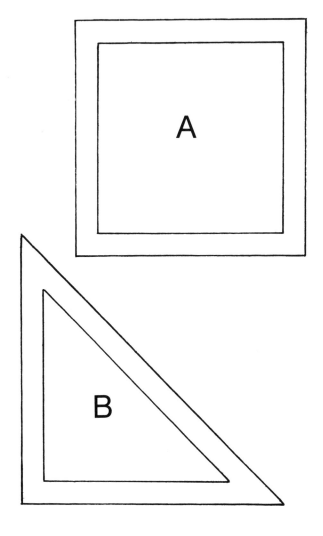

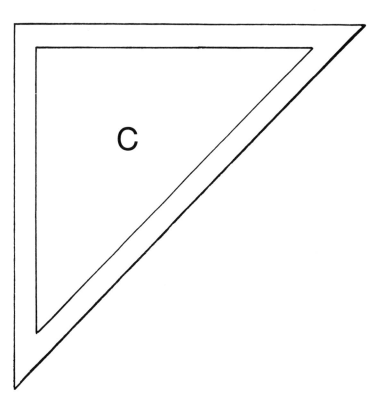

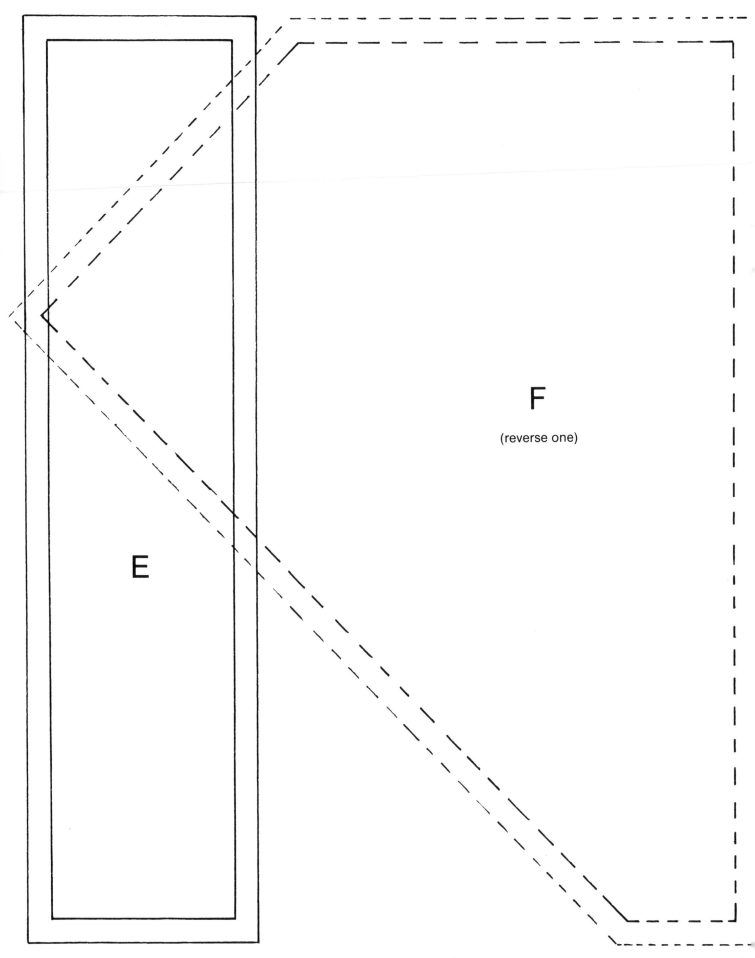

E

F

(reverse one)

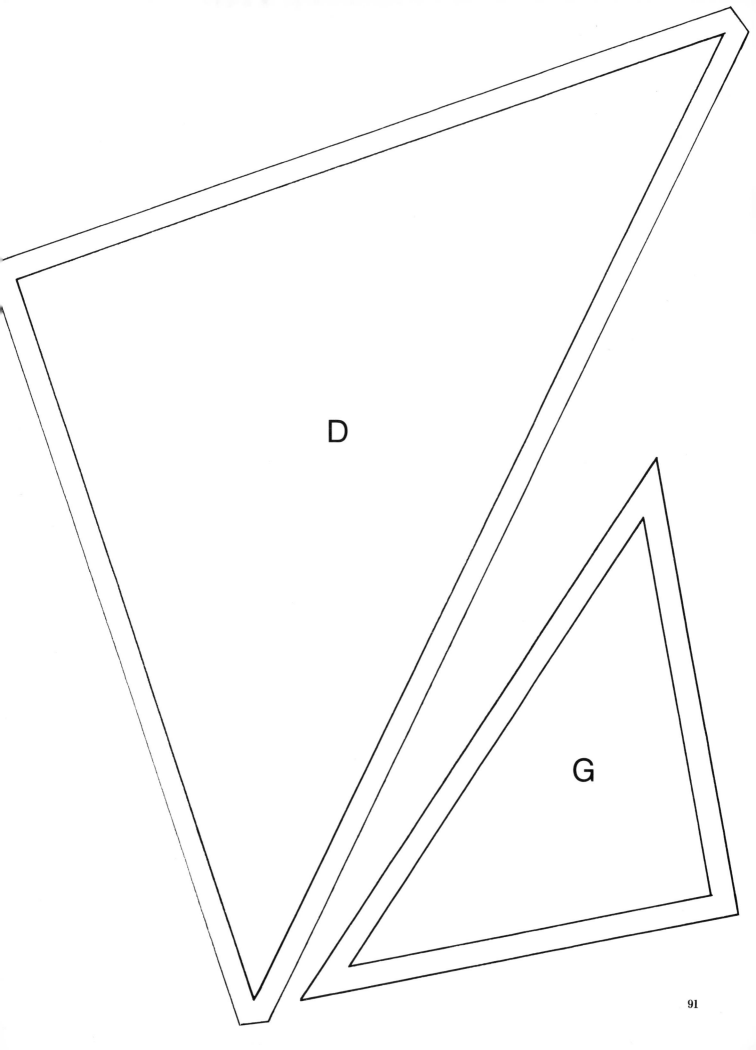

D

G

ATTIC WINDOWS

2-inch, 3-inch, and 4-inch blocks

Attic Windows is a simple block to sew: three seams and you're finished! Templates for three sizes of the pattern have been included for you to choose from.

For each block, cut:

1 of template A dark
1 of template B light
1 of template B *reversed*, medium

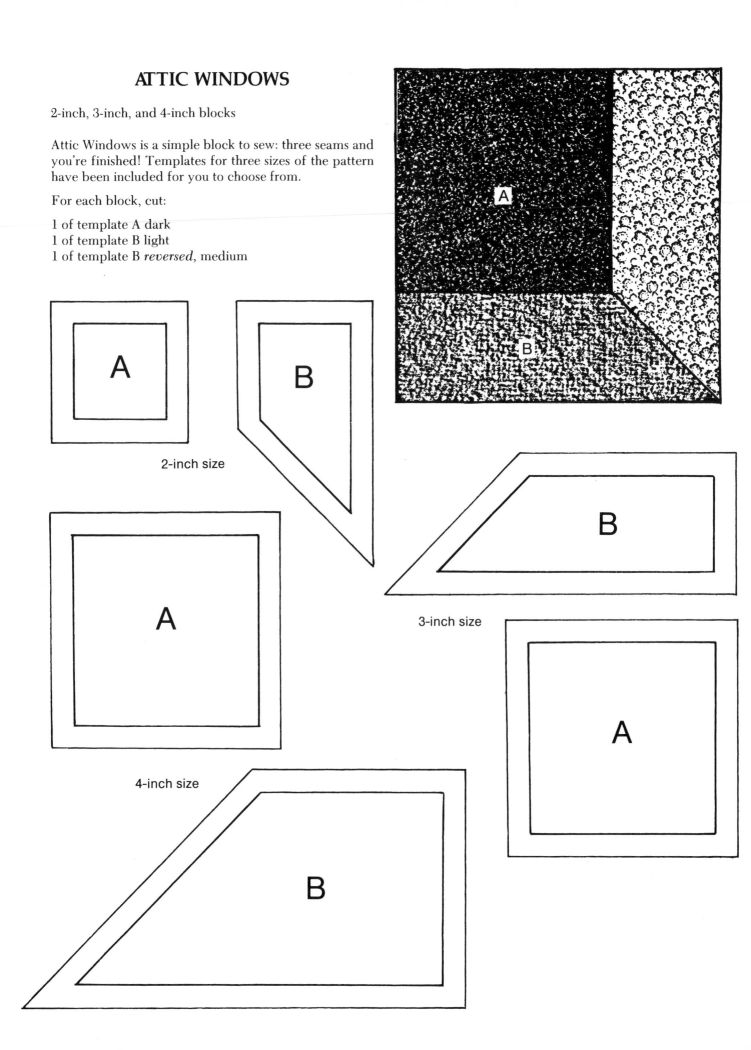

2-inch size

3-inch size

4-inch size

JACOB'S LADDER

12-inch-square block

So easy to assemble, so attractive to look at...that's what you'll think as you're piecing this three-color quilt! Whether the blocks are set together edge to edge, or with lattice strips to separate, the Jacob's Ladder is a wonderful quilt.

For each block, cut:

10 of template A light
10 of template A medium
4 of template B light
4 of template B dark

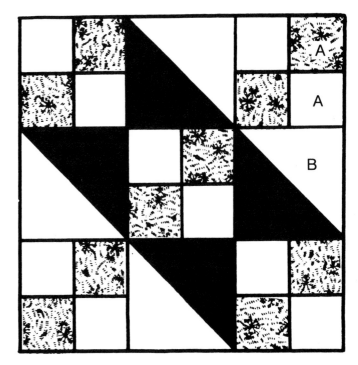

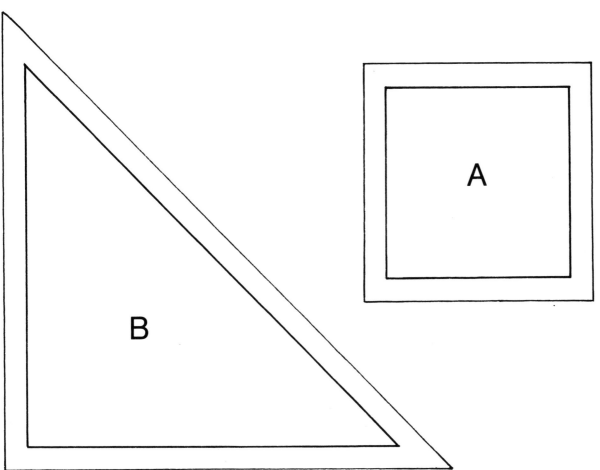

KANSAS DUGOUT

8-inch-square block

The Kansas Dugout block looks more difficult than it actually is. Four miters around each square form the light areas of the block, with triangles sewn in to square off the corners. Two colors could be used throughout, or if desired, a different fabric could be used in each square, turning it into a "charm quilt."

For each block, cut:

4 of template A dark
4 of template B dark
16 of template C light
5 of template D dark

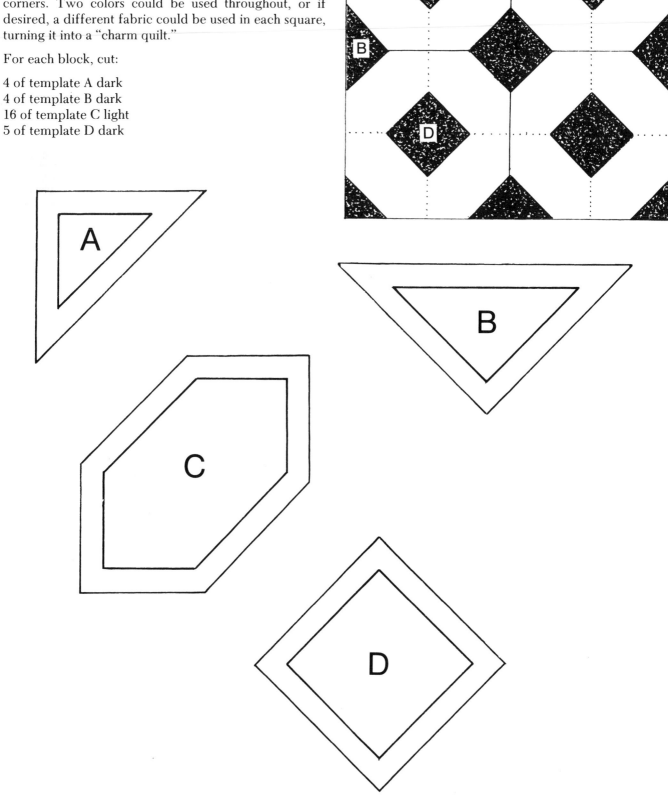

RAIL FENCE

9-inch-square block

If you can cut a rectangle, you can make a quilt in the Rail Fence pattern. The version shown here is similar to that used on the traditional Rail Fence quilt on page 24. Three strips are sewn together forming a square, then four squares are stitched together forming the block.

For each block, cut:

4 of template A dark
4 of template A medium
4 of template A light

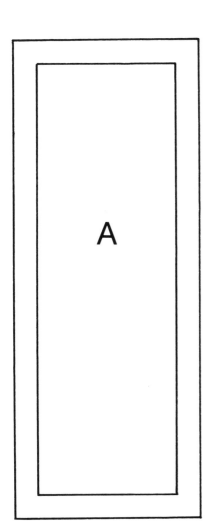

MARINER'S COMPASS

14-inch block: *advanced pattern!*

The Mariner's Compass is probably the most difficult of all patterns shown in this book, due to the number of precise points around the circle. This is a pattern that is best hand-pieced, or machine-pieced following hand-piecing techniques. The templates shown below do *not* include a seam allowance. In hand-piecing, the sewing line is drawn on the *wrong* side of the fabric, and a *quarter-inch-wide seam allowance* is added as each piece is cut out. When stitching, place the patches right sides together and, using a few straight pins, match points. Sew along the drawn line making sure you are catching the line on the underneath side. Seams may be trimmed after sewing.

For each block, cut:

4 of template A
16 of template B
8 of template C
4 of template D
1 of template E
1 of template F

To use template F, fold a 15-inch square of paper into fourths. Trace template F from the book on the folded paper, matching fold lines. Leaving paper folded, cut carefully on the lines you have drawn. Using cut paper as your template, trace on the 15-inch fabric square, remembering to add seam allowances as you cut.

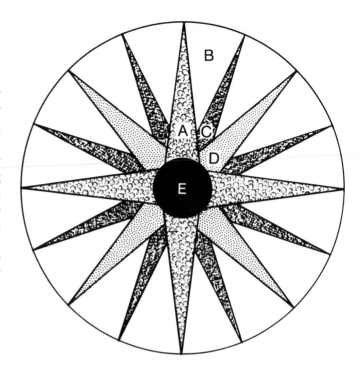

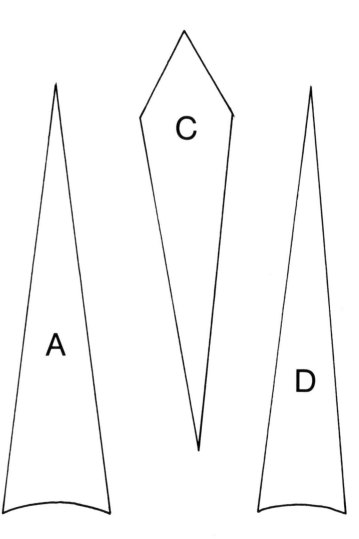

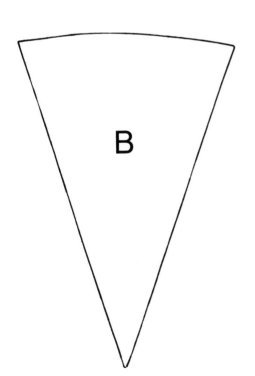

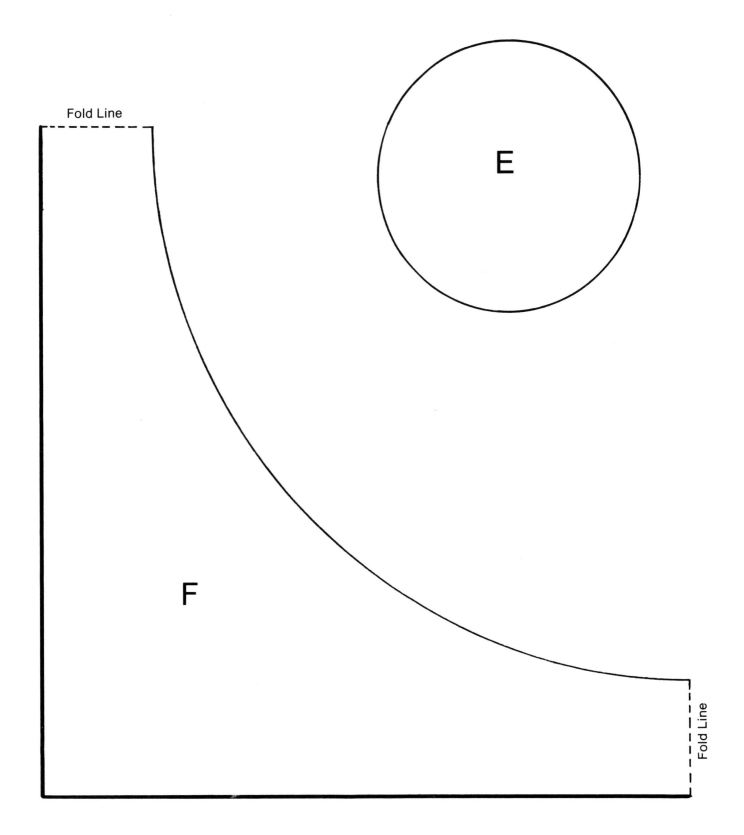

Fold Line

E

F

Fold Line

BIBLIOGRAPHY

Bacon, Lenice Ingram. *American Patchwork Quilts.* New York: Wm. Morrow & Co., Inc., 1973.

Beyer, Jinny. *The Quilter's Album of Blocks and Borders.* McLean, Va.: EPM Publications, Inc., 1980.

———.*The Art and Technique of Creating Medallion Quilts.* McLean, Va.: EPM Publications, Inc., 1982.

Bishop, Robert. *New Discoveries in American Quilts.* New York: E.P. Dutton & Co., 1975.

Bishop, Robert, and Carter Houck. *All Flags Flying: American Patriotic Quilts as Expressions of Liberty.* New York: E.P. Dutton, 1986.

Bonesteel, Georgia. *Lap Quilting.* Birmingham: Oxmoor House, Inc., 1982.

Chase, Pattie, and Mimi Dolbier. *The Contemporary Quilt: New American Quilts and Fabric Art.* New York: E.P. Dutton, Inc., 1978.

Colby, Averil. *Patchwork Quilts.* London: B.T. Batsford, Ltd., 1965.

Cooper, Patricia, and Norma Bradley Buferd. *The Quilters: Women and Domestic Art.* New York: Anchor Press/ Doubleday, 1978.

Finley, Ruth. *Old Patchwork Quilts and the Women Who Made Them.* Newton Center, Mass.: Charles T. Branford Co., 1971.

Fox, Sandi. The Seibu Museum of Art. *19th Century American Patchwork Quilt.* Japan: The Seibu Museum of Art, 1983.

Gutcheon, Beth. *The Perfect Patchwork Primer.* New York: Penguin Books, 1974.

Gutcheon, Beth, and Jeffrey. *The Quilt Design Workbook.* New York: Rawson Associates Publishers, Inc., 1976.

Haders, Phyllis. *Quilts.* Pittstown, N.J.: The Main Street Press, 1981.

———. *Sunshine and Shadow: The Amish and Their Quilts.* New York: The Main Street Press, 1976.

Hall, Carrie, and Rose G. Kretsinger. *The Romance of the Patchwork Quilt in America.* New York: Bonanza Books, 1935.

Hassel, Carla J. *You Can Be a Super Quilter!* Des Moines, Iowa: Wallace Homestead, 1980.

———. *Super Quilter II.* Des Moines, Iowa: Wallace Homestead, 1982.

Hinson, Dolores. *Quilting Manual.* New York: Dover Publications, Inc., 1966.

Holstein, Jonathan. *The Pieced Quilt: An American Design Tradition.* New York: Galahad Books, 1973.

Holstein, Jonathan, and John Finley. *Kentucky Quilts, 1800– 1900.* Louisville, Ky.: The Kentucky Quilt Project, Inc., 1982.

Houck, Carter, and Myron Miller. *American Quilts and How to Make Them.* New York: Charles Scribner's Sons, 1975.

Ickis, Marguerite. *The Standard Book of Quilt Making and Collecting.* New York: Dover Publications, Inc., 1949.

Irwin, John Rice. *A People and Their Quilts.* Exton, Pa.: Schiffer Publishing Ltd., 1983.

James Michael. *The Second Quiltmaker's Handbook: Creative Approaches to Contemporary Quilt Design.* Englewood Cliffs, N.J.:Prentice-Hall, Inc., 1980.

Khin, Yvonne M. *Quilt Names and Patterns.* Washington, D.C.: Acropolis Books, Ltd., 1980.

Kiracofe, Roderick, and Michael Kile. *The Quilt Digest.* San Francisco: Kiracofe and Kile, 1983.

———. *The Quilt Digest.* San Francisco: Kiracofe and Kile, 1984.

Lady's Circle Patchwork Quilts. New York: Lopez Publications.

Leathers, Millie. *First, Nine & Always.* Paducah, Ky.: American Quilter's Society, 1986.

Little, Francis. *Early American Textiles.* New York.: The Century Co., 1931.

Malone, Maggie. *1001 Patchwork Designs.* New York: Sterling Publishing Co., Inc., 1942.

Marston, Gwen. *The Mary Schafer Quilt Collection.* Privately published catalogue, 1980.

McKim, Ruby Short. *One Hundred and One Patchwork Patterns.* New York: Dover Publications, Inc., 1962.

McMorris, Penny. *Crazy Quilts.* New York: E.P. Dutton, Inc., 1984.

Mosey, Caron L. *America's Pictorial Quilts.* Paducah, Ky.: American Quilter's Society, 1985.

Nelson, Cyril I., and Carter Houck. *The Quilt Engagement Calendar Treasury.* New York: E.P. Dutton, Inc., 1982.

Orlofsky, Patsy, and Myron. *Quilts in America.* New York: McGraw-Hill Book Company, 1974.

Pasquini, Katie. *Mandala.* Eureka, Calif.: Sudz Publishing, 1983.

Pellman, Rachel T., and Joanne Ranck. *Quilts Among the Plain People.* Lancaster, Pa.: Good Books, 1981.

Peto, Florence. *American Quilts & Coverlets.* New York: Chanticleer Press, 1949.

Pottinger, David. *Quilts from the Indiana Amish: A Regional Collection*. New York: E.P. Dutton, Inc., 1983.

Quilt Magazine. New York: Harris Publications.

Quilt National. *The Quilt: New Directions for an American Tradition*. Exton Pa.: Schiffer Publishing Ltd., 1983.

———. *Quilts: The State of an Art*. Exton, Pa.: Schiffer Publishing Ltd., 1985.

Robinson, Charlotte. *The Artist & the Quilt*. New York: Alfred A. Knopf, Inc., Quarto Marketing Ltd., 1983.

Safford, Carleton L., and Robert Bishop. *America's Quilts and Coverlets*. New York: Weathervane Books, 1972.

Schlotzhauer, Joyce M. *The Curved Two-Patch System*. McLean, Va.: EPM Publications, 1982.

Simms, Ami. *How to Improve Your Quilting Stitch*. Privately published, 1986.

———. *Invisible Appliqué*. Privately published, 1986.

———. *Little Ditties*. Privately published, 1986.

Texas Heritage Quilt Society. *Texas Quilts, Texas Treasures*. Paducah, Ky.: American Quilter's Society, 1986.

Tomlonson, Judy Schroeder. *Mennonite Quilts and Pieces*. Intercourse, Pa.: Good Books, 1985.

Woodard, Thos. K., and Blanche Greenstein. *Crib Quilts and Other Small Wonders*. New York: E.P. Dutton, 1981.

World of Quilts at Meadowbrook Hall. Oakland University. Privately published catalogue, copyright 1983 by Marylin Brooks.

INDEX

Caron L. Mosey is the author of *America's Pictorial Quilts*, and she is currently serving as Contributing Editor to *Quilt Magazine*. As a member of the National Writer's Club, she has written over fifty freelance articles on quilting and collecting quilts and antiques. Her quilts have received numerous blue ribbons, and she keeps busy teaching and lecturing across the United States.

Additional copies of *Contemporary Quilts from Traditional Designs* may be purchased directly from the author at the following address:

Caron L. Mosey
191 Park Avenue
Flushing, Michigan
48433